Minot Judson Savage

Life Beyond Death

Being a review of the world's beliefs on the subject, a consideration of present conditions of thought and feeling, leading to the question as to whether it can be demonstrated as a fact

Minot Judson Savage

Life Beyond Death
Being a review of the world's beliefs on the subject, a consideration of present conditions of thought and feeling, leading to the question as to whether it can be demonstrated as a fact

ISBN/EAN: 9783337403195

Printed in Europe, USA, Canada, Australia, Japan

Cover: Foto ©Thomas Meinert / pixelio.de

More available books at **www.hansebooks.com**

LIFE BEYOND DEATH

BEING A REVIEW OF THE WORLD'S BELIEFS ON THE SUBJECT, A CONSIDERATION OF PRESENT CONDITIONS OF THOUGHT AND FEELING, LEADING TO THE QUESTION AS TO WHETHER IT CAN BE DEMON- STRATED AS A FACT

TO WHICH IS ADDED

AN APPENDIX CONTAINING SOME HINTS AS TO PERSONAL EXPERIENCES AND OPINIONS

BY

MINOT JUDSON SAVAGE, D.D. (HARVARD)

G. P. PUTNAM'S SONS
NEW YORK & LONDON
The Knickerbocker Press
1899

TO PHILIP HENRY SAVAGE

FEBRUARY 11, 1868—JUNE 4, 1899

My dear Phil:

As you are the first one of our family circle to go into the "Life Beyond Death," it seems peculiarly fitting that I should let my love have its way, and dedicate to you this, my attempt to find the entrance to that mist-covered harbour of which all the world has dreamed, and which the true lovers and high thinkers of every age have sought. I am grateful, even to tears, for our thirty-one years together—even though that should be all. But let my pride in you have way for a moment, while I set down a record which I believe the world can rarely match. Never was finger of father or mother laid on you except in the way of caress. Never was there one hour of misunderstanding between us. Never did you give us one hour of anxiety. Never did you speak a word to us, nor we to

iii

you, which we would now forget. One more thing let me say. Never knew I a braver going. Never read I of one. From perfect health— as we all supposed—you went into the shadow in full strength, and inside of three days. With a poetic promise fully recognised; with most of those you loved, including her you were to marry, by your hospital bedside; with worldly prosperity in sight; with all the thrilling life and hope of youth,—you faced the shadow with all tenderest words of love for all of us, but with not one selfish syllable on your lips. You did not even complain that it was hard to turn away from all you loved, for a future concerning which you claimed to know nothing, and in which you had no strongly assured faith. "I do not need any more help; I can go on alone." With such words, you stepped over the border, and found—as I fully believe —a clearer light and a grander life. I shall do better work henceforth because you are one of the "great cloud of witnesses." And, as I dreamed the other night, when my time comes to go, I shall look for your face as the first to break through the mist, as I cross the bar, and come to anchor in the world-desired haven. I believe you will henceforth watch over us, help us as you are able, be preparing a place for us;

and the going will be easier, for us who hold you in our hearts, because you are there. God bless you, my boy, till the eyes which I closed I see open again and looking into mine.

Lovingly,

FATHER.

Signed at the town of Billerica, Massachusetts, every spot of which was dear to the passionate Nature-lover and Nature-poet.

September, 1899.

PREFACE

A NEWSPAPER article which I came across the other day suggests the necessity for the kind of preface which is offered to the reader. The writer was a physician, and so might presumably claim to understand the " scientific method." The position he assumed was that there was no possibility of scientific demonstration in the matter of psychical research. The argument was meant to be fair and, by many, might be regarded as conclusive. As some parts of this book will be open to this kind of attack, I wish to state the writer's argument (of course in my own words, but I hope fairly), and then see if it is valid.

He claimed that nothing could be demonstrated scientifically unless the matter involved could be submitted to satisfactory tests by anybody, at any time, and with the certainty of immediate uniform results. This is undoubtedly true of the scientific method when dealing with inanimate forces or things. But is it true in dealing with living beings —with men and women ?

I have been accustomed to think and say for many years that " the scientific method " is the only method of knowledge. What does this mean ? It means that whatever one may feel or think or

believe or regard as probable he does not *know* unless
it is capable of demonstration in accordance with
the scientific method.

Let us note the steps of progress in the scientific
method so that this matter may be made clear to
any intelligent reader whether scientific or not.

1. The first step is *observation*. I open my eyes
(whether outer or inner) and see a fact. This
proves nothing beyond my own personal impression.
If I am colour-blind or ignorant or prejudiced, my
seeing may be incorrect and so not correspond to
any reality.

2. So there must be *repeated* observation and
corroborative observation on the part of others.

3. Then, after a number of facts appear to be
satisfactorily determined, a tentative theory may be
formed in accordance with these facts. This is what
science means by the " process of induction." But
this theory is always open to revision, provided
other facts are discovered which are not in accord
with the theory. The " law of parsimony " demands also that the nearest and easiest theory
which will explain the facts shall have the prefer-
ence. That is, a strained or far-fetched theory
must not be dragged in where the facts can be explained by an easier or more " natural " method.

4. When a large number of facts are satisfactorily
established and all or most of them can be most
easily explained in the light of some particular
theory, that theory is regarded as scientifically
established. This, for instance, is the case to-day
in regard to the Copernican theory of the universe.

The theory of evolution and the nebular theory are also cases in point. It is conceivable that either of these might be overthrown or essentially modified by the discovery of a sufficient number of new facts which could not be explained in accordance with them. Professor See, for example, is calling in question certain phases of the nebular theory. But the facts must be many and important before a man is justified in demanding that a well-established theory be given up. He must be sure that he is not misinterpreting his facts.

Now I submit that this, the scientific method, can be followed in observing and proving anything which is real and which touches us, and so comes into the field of observation. But while a man can *command* the action of certain forces and *order* the conduct of his observations in his laboratory; or while he may count on the absolute uniformity of the motions of the heavenly bodies, there are other facts, and those of far greater importance, which he cannot treat in this way, although he may still be true to the scientific method. You cannot *order people round*, as a chemist may his elements, and yet facts concerning people may be scientifically demonstrated. The same thing is true of the people in the other life—provided there are any. It is conceivable that "a spirit" may be present and communicate in certain circumstances. Identity even may conceivably be established. And yet the precise experiment one may not be able to repeat *at will*, for the simple but satisfactory reason that, *ex hypothesi, another will* is concerned; the person may not be present the next time; he is not under orders; and the conditions may not be capable of duplication by anybody who happens to come along.

The Society for Psychical Research is engaged in the task of investigating a large body of facts, whatever may ultimately be regarded as the explanation of them. Several different explanations have been offered. The principal ones are these:

1. Fraud.

2. Auto-suggestion: that is, that the sitter unintentionally " gives himself away "—as the phrase goes. He unconsciously imparts the information which so astonishes him when he gets it back again.

I have seen a great deal of both of these.

3. That the facts are the work of the subconscious mind of either the sitters, the psychic, or all together.

4. Mind-reading or telepathy.

5. The " spirit " theory. This means, of course, that persons who have " died " and are now in the life which is ordinarily regarded as the abode of silence and invisibility can and do (at least occasionally) manifest their presence and communicate their thoughts.

Now, in the first place, it can be settled as to whether any of these claimed facts are facts. Then, in the second place, it can be determined as to whether any one of these theories can explain the facts. If it can, then it would be provisionally established as a scientific hypothesis, in precisely the same sense that the Copernican theory of the universe is established, and with as scientific a

validity. Like that, it would still be liable to
question or revision, provided new facts should
arise which it could not find place for. And conceivably it might be displaced altogether, provided
a more satisfactory theory should present itself.
But meantime it would rightly claim the intelligent
acceptance of all educated and free minds.

I submit then to all competent thinkers that the
psychical problems can be scientifically investigated,
and that a true scientific theory concerning them can
be framed and verified.

M. J. S.

September 16, 1899.

CONTENTS

CHAPTER   PAGE

I.—PRIMITIVE IDEAS . 1

II.—ETHNIC BELIEFS 19

III.—THE OLD TESTAMENT AND IMMORTALITY . 41

IV.—PAUL'S DOCTRINE OF DEATH AND THE OTHER LIFE . . . 63

V.—JESUS AND IMMORTALITY 88

VI.—THE OTHER WORLD AND THE MIDDLE AGES 111

VII.—PROTESTANT BELIEF CONCERNING DEATH AND THE LIFE BEYOND . . 133

VIII.—THE AGNOSTIC REACTION . . . 156

IX.—THE SPIRITUALISTIC REACTION . . 178

X.—THE WORLD'S CONDITION AND NEEDS AS TO BELIEF IN IMMORTALITY . . . 200

XI.—PROBABILITIES WHICH FALL SHORT OF DEMONSTRATION 222

XII.—THE SOCIETY FOR PSYCHICAL RESEARCH AND THE IMMORTAL LIFE . . . 245

XIII.—POSSIBLE CONDITIONS OF ANOTHER LIFE . 271

APPENDIX.—SOME HINTS AS TO PERSONAL EXPERIENCES AND OPINIONS . . . 295

THE MYSTIC HOPE.

What is this mystic, wondrous hope in me,
That, when no star from out the darkness born
Gives promise of the coming of the morn;
When all life seems a pathless mystery
Through which tear-blinded eyes no way can see;
When illness comes, and life grows most forlorn,
Still dares to laugh the last dread threat to scorn,
And proudly cries, Death is not, shall not be?

I wonder at myself! Tell me, O Death,
If that thou rul'st the earth; if " dust to dust "
Shall be the end of love and hope and strife,
From what rare land is blown this living breath
That shapes itself to whispers of strong trust
And tells the lie—if 't is a lie—of life?

M. J. S.

xv

LIFE BEYOND DEATH

PRIMITIVE IDEAS

IT is said that, when Henry D. Thoreau lay
dying in Concord, his friend Parker Pills-
bury sat by his bedside ; and he leaned over,
and took him by the hand, and said, " Henry,
you are so near to the border now, can you see
anything on the other side ? " And Thoreau
answered, " One world at a time, Parker."

It has seemed to a great many that this answer is wisdom. I cannot so take it. The
human race never will surrender this quest
until, one way or the other, it is settled. We
cannot take one world at a time. Why ?
There are two or three answers which I would
suggest.

In the first place, on the reply to this query,
" If a man die, shall he live again ? " depends
our answer to the question : What kind of a

being is man ? What am I ? The Greek wise man said that the most important item of all knowledge was to know one's self. We cannot know ourselves until we know whether the grave is the end of us or not. Is there something in us that overleaps the gulf we call death, that continues through the dissolution of the body ? Do we end when what we call life ends, or do we simply keep on ? Is Death the extinguisher of life, or is he the great gate-opener, letting us out into larger fields, into wider and grander opportunities ? Until I know whether or no there is something in me that Death cannot touch or destroy, I cannot know what sort of a person I am.

In the second place, until I can find out what sort of person I am, how am I going to determine an answer to the question as to how I ought to live ? The kind of life appropriate to a bird or to an animal of any sort depends entirely upon the nature, the faculties, the possibilities, of that bird or animal. What it can become or accomplish, it ought to become or accomplish, we say. Now what can man do ? What can man become ? What can he accomplish ?

We cannot answer that question until we can find out approximately what sort of being man is. Shall I live simply as an animal? Not at my peril, if I am something else than an animal, something more than an animal. Is wealth or fame or pleasure the appropriate end and object of human life? That depends upon what a man is, what a man is capable of doing and being. So, for the sake of finding out what kind of life a man ought to lead, we need to know whether he is a soul or whether he is only a body.

The whole question of the emphasis of morals is to be determined right here. If I decide that, when I come to the grave, I am to lie down in an age-long sleep, that does not make right wrong, or wrong right : it does not therefore become proper for me to steal, or to cheat, or to lie, to take advantage of my neighbour. But where I shall place the emphasis of my moral life, and how much I shall think it worth my while to try to accomplish or to become,— the answer to these questions depends vitally upon my opinion as to whether my life leads out into something beyond the grave or not.

To illustrate : If I know that, after I have lived ten years here, that is the end of me, one kind of life would be appropriate to me. If I know that at the end of ten or twenty years I am going suddenly to be transferred to some other country, to some other kind of life, in the midst of other kinds of people, have other ambitions and cares, and that the life I am leading here is of no particular account except as a preparation for that, and that that is to continue indefinitely, do you not see that it changes the whole problem as to where I am to place the emphasis of my life?

One other point I wish to suggest : I believe that the solution of our industrial and social problems depends more than almost anything else upon our answer to this question as to what is the nature of man, and what is his destiny. Those who have made a careful study of these questions already warn us that the Socialists are saying :

"It used to be the Church and the nobility, now it is the Church and the *bourgeoisie ;* and in either case they are telling us to be contented with the lot in which Providence has chosen to place us, and to look for our consolation in some other life. That is what they have always been telling us. Now we do not believe in any other life, and we propose to have our share of the good things of the world as they go."

That is only Paul's logic. "If the dead rise not," Paul says, "let us eat and drink ; for to-morrow we die." That is what the Socialists are saying. If there is no future life, we are going to claim our share of the good things here. And if this life is only a larger dog-kennel, if we are shut in under "this inverted bowl men call the sky," and, when we get through here, that is the end of it,—if that is true, tell me why some fortunate member of the canine race should sit and guard a pile of bones a thousand times larger than he can eat, while I simply whine and starve?

If there is another life, if this is only preparation; if we are not bodies, but souls, and are cultivating our souls through the discipline of life's experiences here for that infinite career which opens through the gateway of death,—then that is one thing. It may be worth while, then, to be poor; it may be worth while to want, to suffer, to go through any experience, so I be true to myself. But, if the time ever comes when the great masses of the world have made up their minds that all there is to human life is right here, then look to your social order; and, with Paul's word as authority, they can demand their little share of something to eat and drink before the to-morrow comes when they are to die.

These are some hints as to the reasons why, in my opinion, we cannot take one world at a time. The question as to whether there is another world makes all imaginable difference as to what we shall think about, and how we shall use, this one.

One or two other preliminary thoughts need to be touched on briefly. There are large numbers of people who tell us that this is a problem impossible of solution; that we can hope and dream as much as we please, but we shall never be able to know. I have had this told me, I suppose, a thousand times when I have been discussing the matter. But the world has done so many "impossible" things that I do not despair even of this. We are not in the temper now to have wise people draw lines beyond which they say we cannot go. The great French philosopher Comte tried it. He said it was no use trying to study the nature of the fixed stars; that was something forever beyond the reach of the human intellect. But he had hardly been buried before the spectroscope was discovered; and we know all about them now. A man in England said that a steamship could not cross the Atlantic Ocean; and his demonstration was hardly completed when a ship did come over, and brought that demonstration with it.

So we are not in a temper to be very patient with the people who tell us it is impossible to do this or that or the other thing. We will decide that it is impossible when there is no avenue of investigation or study that is left to us.

There are others who tell us that it is better that we should not know. I wonder how they found that out? They say that moral action must have in it an element of faith, of uncertainty. If you are sure of the result of what you do, the moral quality is taken out of it. I could never quite see why. A thing is good, even if I know that it is good. It is not necessary that I should have a doubt about it, in order to create a moral quality.

Then there are those who tell us that there would be a rapid increase of suicides if we were perfectly certain about the other life,—that men would not bear the burdens that crush them down if they knew that death was not the end. Rather do I think that the number of suicides would decrease if we knew, first, that life keeps on ; and, if we knew, secondly, that under the universal law of cause and effect we are creating the to-morrow of death by the way in which we live the to-day of life. Rather do I believe that men would learn patiently to bear almost anything if they knew that the outcome was to be something certain, and that it might possibly be high and fine if they chose to make it so.

So I believe that this hope that there is something better awaiting us across the border, if it can be transformed from hope to an absolute certainty, would be a grand gain in the upward lift of the life of man.

There is one other thing that people are saying to us constantly,—I have had it said to me innumerable times,—" If God had intended that we should know, He would have made it perfectly plain to us." Why does not that principle apply to every other item of knowledge as well? If God had intended that Europe should know there was another continent over here to the west, He would have made it perfectly plain, and not left the world to wonder and speculate and venture for several thousand years before they found it out.

As a matter of fact, God has not directly told us anything. He has left us to study and investigate on our own account, and to develop and cultivate our own intellectual and moral and spiritual natures in this process of study and investigation.

So much by way of prelude. Let us turn now to consider briefly—for it will require no very profound investigation — the ideas of death and after which were held by primitive men.

You know the Catholic Church tells us that Catholic doctrine is held with absolute certainty because all men always and everywhere have believed it. In other words, that which has been always believed by all men everywhere is true. So it may be important for us, in view of this assertion, to find out what the ideas of primitive man were on so important a subject as this.

But can we get at primitive man? Those who know, or think they know, tell us that men have been on this planet for something like three or four hundred thousand years.

How then can we get at the thoughts of primitive men? We cannot, in one sense; and yet, so far as all practical necessity is concerned, we can. We need to remember that there are men to-day on the islands of the sea and in distant parts of the world who are living in a stage of culture which represents man's life two hundred thousand years ago. And we are to remember that these first men progressed very slowly. And we are to remember, further, that religion, as we are finding out by constant experience every day of our lives, is the last thing in the world that anybody is ever willing to change. Men hold it as so sacred that they hesitate to touch or change a religious belief or ritual or habit. So that for all practical purposes we can get at the primitive ideas of man concerning death and another life.

It seems to me one of the strangest, one of the most startling things in the world, that men should have ever dreamed of another life at all. We stand beside a casket containing the body of a friend. That mysterious something that we call life is gone. That which looked out of the eyes, that which shaped the viewless air into speech on the lips, that which was in the clasp of the hand, that which animated the feet on their errands of kindliness and mercy, —life,—is gone. And it certainly does seem as though this were the end. And so I say it seems to me one of the most startling, audacious imaginations that ever entered the mind of man. Whence did it come,—the dream that something lives after death ? Some very remarkable thing must have happened along the lines of evolution between the highest animal and the lowest man. Animals think, dream, reason. Animals are conscious ; but animals are not self-conscious. No dog ever says, I am a dog, and thinks out the difference between himself and other kinds of animals. If we should once see a Newfoundland dog gazing at the body of a comrade, weeping tears of heartbreak and saying to himself, " If a dog die, shall he live again ? " we should think we were in the presence of some strange phenomenon, something more than we associate with animal life. And yet the lowest man that has ever been found on the face of the earth has not only asked this question, but has always answered it in the affirmative.

One of the most striking things is to note that primitive men never believe in natural death. When a man dies, they feel perfectly certain that somebody has killed him ; it is an enemy. If not an enemy in the body, then a malignant spirit or one of the gods. This is the point I wish you to note : that primitive man does not believe in natural death. He believes that it is always caused by somebody; that it cannot be natural, a part of any order of things. Indeed he has no idea of any order of things.

Now it is very natural that a crude, ignorant being should give very unsatisfactory reasons for his belief. Primitive man, wherever he can be found, always believes in a spiritual and an ordinarily invisible existence ; but the reasons that he would give you for holding that belief might be very crude and ignorant. It is, on the face of it, very strange and startling that it should be believed at all.

The origin of the belief is still a matter of dispute among scholars. A certain class of thinkers associate it with shadows and dreams and swoons; and very likely they may be right. Primeval man has no idea of the laws of reflection of light; and he sees himself sometimes accompanied by a shadowy, secondary self that comes in a mysterious fashion and goes away, he does not know how. He bends over a pool or a running stream, and sees this shadowy, secondary self there again, the one he had seen in the sunlight. It comes and goes in a wonderful way, he knows not why. Then he lies down when he is tired, and goes to sleep; and he is off on a journey. He visits friends, he fights with his enemies, he is engaged in the delights and excitements of the chase. By and by he comes to himself, he wakes up; and why should not this dream experience seem to him as real as any other? But his comrades tell him that his body has been here all the time, has not moved. Then he straightway reasons, it is this spiritual, shadowy, secondary self that has been off on these excursions, engaged in these different occupations.

And then, in the case of swoons, perhaps an enemy strikes him with a club, and he loses consciousness. His friends would not be able to tell that from death except that in one case this secondary self returns, and in the other it does not. We have still kept, in our civilised and modern speech, the last pale remnant of that old idea. A friend faints; and, as she is recovering consciousness, we say, " She is coming to." She is coming back to the body that she had temporarily left. That is what the phrase means.

And who shall tell us whether these primitive men were right or wrong? No philosopher, no scientist, on the face of the earth is as yet able to explain to us either sleep or dream. There are those who believe that in sleep the spirit does temporarily leave the body, as an engineer leaves his engine for a little time, while he oils it and coals it and gets it ready to run its course again. There are men, I say, in the modern world, who believe this; and there is nobody wise enough to convince them that they are wrong. It is a matter concerning which we have no definite knowledge one way or the other.

But the point you need to note and bear in mind is that primitive man, by some process of reasoning, came to accept the belief that he did have a secondary self inside his body, which could exist apart from his body, and which could go and come as a man leaves his house and returns to it again, and which, when death came to the body, went to return no more; but did not cease to exist.

Now there are one or two points connecting this idea with modern religious beliefs and practices which I must notice briefly.

The first altar was undoubtedly a grave; for, believing that their dead friends continued to exist, they naturally reasoned that they continued to hunger and thirst just as they did here. So they brought and poured out on the grave drink for them, and laid upon it food, believing that then they ate the spiritual essence, knowing of course that the substance which they could see and handle was not thus consumed. A precisely similar idea, however, to this, enters into the philosophy of the Eucharist as it is held in the Catholic Church to-day.

The chants that were gone through with, in celebration of the virtues and heroic qualities of the dead, have their modern representative undoubtedly in our hymns of praise. They prayed to the dead, because they believed that these invisible friends or enemies were all about them in the air, and could help them or hurt them at will. They lighted fires on graves to show the soul the pathway through the dark in its journey to its other home; and in certain churches of the modern world candles are lighted and placed at the head of the casket; and the one is vitally, intimately, connected with the other. The candle is only the civilised and modern representative of the primitive man's fire, which was to light the way of the soul on its dark journey.

That which at first was only food and drink for the dead developed later into sacrifice; and this sacrifice at first was a communion meal, of which the god partook along with his worshippers. Then, later still, it became an offering of thanks or of propitiation. The Eucharist, which did not originate with Christianity, is the last and present representative of this primeval custom.

Where did they believe that these souls went after death? At first they would naturally haunt the places to which they had been accustomed while living, and so it was believed that they were all about them; and, if they were enemies, they prayed to be delivered from their power, tried to propitiate their wrath. If they were friends, they rejoiced in their presence, and expected from them guidance and help. But by and by a tribe would move from its old habitat. Perhaps it first lived at the mouth of a river, and afterwards it would wander up the course of this river a hundred or two hundred miles; and then they would think of the soul of the dead as going back to the old home. That is one of the most tender and touching things connected with this old thought, and is to be found throughout the entire history of the race. The place where the souls go is thought of as home: heaven is home.

So, among these primitive ancestors, after they had wandered up the river, when it came to the time of burial, they would put the body of their friend in a boat, and send it adrift on the tide, so that it might go back to the old home. And, when they had wandered inland, they would still bury the body in a boat, or something bearing the semblance of a boat; so persistent are these religious ideas and practices when once they become a part of the thought and life of the world.

But almost every conceivable place came to

be looked upon after a while, among some of
the primeval peoples, as the abode of the dead.
You remember reading in "Hiawatha" how
the hero sets sail out over a lake in the track of
the setting sun, and goes down towards those
islands of the blessed, which perhaps had been
created out of the clouds made glorious in the
last rays of evening. In northern lands the
glories of the auroral lights have been connected with the homes of departed spirits.
Among other people these spirits have trodden
the path of the Milky Way to some far place
in the sky. Among other people there has
been an abode beneath the surface of the earth.
A thousand shapes this imaginative, loving
trust of the world has taken, providing places
where every want would be satisfied, where the
tears should be all wiped away, where was to
be no more sorrow, no more care, no more
trouble, where every instinctive wish and desire
should find its legitimate satisfaction.

It is important to note—and we shall find the
same truth all the way along—that primitive
men believed in the possibility of communication between the two worlds.

No matter what the form may have been
that these dreams and hopes have assumed,
the one thing that I wish to impress upon you,

as of more importance than anything else, is the simple fact that the very earliest men of the world *should have believed.*   I think there is no exception : no tribe so ignorant, so degraded, so low, so uncultured, has been found that it did not hold in some form the belief that there was that in man which death could not touch.

Is this delusion, or is it a whisper of the Eternal Spirit suggesting comfort and hope to His mortal children?   Is it a will-o'-the-wisp that plays over marshes that cannot sustain the feet of those that pursue, leading only into darkness and distress; or is it, far away down the pathway of history, beyond the mists that rise over the twilight of the early world, —is it the first glimpse and gleam of a dawn, the dawn of a day that is destined to grow brighter and brighter until all darkness has disappeared?

ETHNIC BELIEFS

NO one will expect me to undertake the impossible task of compressing, or trying to compress, within the limits of one chapter, any general treatment of so large a theme. My purpose is a much simpler one than this. It is not particularly the belief of Egypt or India or Scandinavia or Greece or Rome that I am interested in. It is the growth and changes in the belief of man; and I wish to consider these merely as phases of this human belief. And so what I have in hand just now is to note in some general way how far along in its progress the world had come when it reached the culmination of these old-time civilisations.

We first treated the ideas of primitive man. This, as you see, is the next step; and after this we shall leave what we are accustomed to call the pagan world, and take up the line of historic progress that goes under the name of Hebrew and Christian civilisation.

At present, then, we are to consider for a little how far the world had gone at the height of the civilisations of these old-time peoples, in its development concerning the belief about death and the life that it supposed was to follow it.

One thing is worthy of our notice. The peoples of these different countries did not look upon this belief as a childish relic of the olden time, as something which barbaric people held, but which was to be outgrown and left behind. We find that the belief among these great nations was practically universal. They all held that death was not the end, but only an incident in life, leading to something beyond. But, when we speak of the belief of Egypt or of India or of any one of these other great nations, we need to keep carefully in mind one fact. Any one of these peoples had had a progress of thousands of years ; and of course its beliefs in regard to these matters, as well as in any other direction, had naturally and necessarily undergone many modifications.

To illustrate what I mean : Suppose I should make some general statement about English belief concerning death and a future life. One might remind me of the fact that there were native Britons on the island before any conquest of which we know ; then that the island was conquered by other peoples, bringing with them their peculiar ideas, which ultimately became amalgamated with the native thought of the old Britons. Then by and by Christianity came and conquered the original Paganism : it was Catholic Christianity. This was followed by the Protestant Revolution ; this by the rise of free thought, the scientific spirit, agnosticism, and all the speculations of modern times. So one might very well ask me, when I refer to English belief, what period of English belief I have in mind ; for there are many English beliefs. But I do not need to do more than take notice of this fact. Let not the reader think I have carelessly over-looked it. It will be enough for my purpose to refer to some general outlines of the faith of these great peoples at certain periods of their most advanced civilisation.

I wish now to make some brief suggestions concerning the nature of the places where the souls of the dead were supposed to have gone. I want, in other words, to bring imaginatively to the eye, if I can, some suggestive and sufficient picture of this other life which these people believed in. I can only set forth a few illustrative hints.

The Egyptian religion is based on and is always connected with astronomical studies; and, when the Egyptians came to believe in these other worlds for the souls of the dead, they connected them popularly with the circuit of the sun. The good souls either accompanied the sun in his progress or lived somewhere along the course of the sun's daily advance, while the bad were connected with his transit through the world of darkness and shadows preparatory to his daily course again.

The Scandinavians had for their heroes and great fighters the Hall of Valhalla, where the souls fought over again the battles in which they so delighted here. They drank the celestial mead, and celebrated their deeds of renown. But this was not the only heaven that the Norsemen knew. They believed in a Hall of Friends, where quiet and gentle souls found an abode of peace. There was a place where the noble women of the world received the reward for their lives of faithfulness and devotion. They also, of course, with all these nations at the highest period of their development, had their places of sorrow and suffering, and sometimes of torture for those who had offended the gods or who had wronged their fellow-men.

The Indian peoples believed in heavens and hells, both located in some indefinite region of space,—heavens where the good rested during the periods that separated the times of their different births. There were also hells where the bad awaited the new and worse fate that was to come to them by being born into some hideous, diseased, or animal form.

The Persians also had their heavens and their hells. The Greeks and the Romans, with whom, perhaps, we are more familiar than with either of these others, located the under-world always beneath the surface of the earth. It was a place to which descent might conceivably be made. Some living person, as in the case of Æneas and Ulysses, might go down and visit those who were the inhabitants of this lower world. It was then always an underground cavern with the classic people where the good and bad went; for, except in the case of some highly favoured souls, semi-divine heroes who were transferred to Olympus and were companions of the gods, no one ever "went to heaven" in the sense in which we are at the present time accustomed to use that term.

These realms, then, as I said, were either under the surface of the earth or off somewhere in the interstellar spaces. But we must bear in mind, if we wish to have any adequate thought of these old-time ideas, that the universe up to within four hundred years of the present time has been comparatively a very small affair. The entire universe as it was thought of by the Greeks and Romans, for example, was not so large, not nearly so large as we imagine the solar system to be. The stars were not so very far away. Heaven was just above the dome of blue. And you are aware of the traditions that made people think that it might be possible for some hero to scale heaven and threaten the stability of the throne of Jupiter himself.

(These merely as hints of the comparative size of the universe in the old time and the present.)

Now I wish to suggest further some peculiar facts in regard to the nature of the soul,— the inhabitants of these other worlds. There are persons at the present time who, under the name of theosophy, have resurrected, or suppose themselves to have resurrected, certain phases of Buddha's Oriental ideas, who talk to us about shells and astral bodies as separate possibly from the central soul of man. It is very curious to note that in Greek and Latin mythology, as well as among the Egyptians and some of the other ancient nations, ideas akin to these were held.

For example, when Ulysses goes down to the underworld, among others that he meets there, is the shade of Hercules ; and this shade is able to talk with him. He has indeed a shadowy life, but substance enough to carry on a conversation with the living hero ; and yet, according to the teaching of the thought of the time, the real Hercules, a demigod, had been transferred to Olympus, and was there living in companionship with the gods. So that, in a certain sense, you see there were two of him.

Among the Egyptians also we find there was an unreal sort of shadow that sometimes haunted the tomb, or in some indefinite way was connected with the mummy, while the real soul was in one of the heavens or hells, receiving the rewards or undergoing the punishments of the life he had lived here below the stars.

Souls, therefore, were somewhat bountifully supplied ; and one of them could be in one place, while another was somewhere else. It reminds us of the Scotch traditions concerning the wraith, or apparition, which may be seen wandering over the heather while the owner is alive, and presumably has his body and soul both with him wherever he may be. But this life which they lived was a very shadowy one. Of course, we cannot reconcile it with any reasonable philosophical speculation of the modern world. When Æneas talks with his father Anchises in this underworld, the old man can weep, can speak in a voice that can be heard. He remembers the past, he forecasts the future ; and yet, when the son endeavours to embrace him, there is no substance there, and his arms pass through the form as if it were merely a shadow.

These people in the underworld, again, are ordinarily supposed to be ignorant of what is taking place on the surface of the earth ; and yet they have not forgotten the past. They are intensely interested in it. They are glad to hear news of their children, their descendants. They are proud if they have attained prosperity. They are cast down with sadness if they do not live lives which they regard as worthy, or, indeed, if anything un-fortunate has befallen them. Ignorant then generally as to what has taken place on the surface of the earth, it is still true—and I wish this to be noted as a separate and distinct fact

—that under special conditions it is believed that communication may be established between the underworld and the world up here where the sun shines. The way is usually closed. It is difficult for a spirit to come up to the surface of the earth. It is difficult for a man to go down and mingle with the shades. But there are conditions in which it is possible. This is worthy of attention, because there never has been a time that we can trace from the beginning of human thought on this subject, when a belief like this has not been held. I do not say now that it is important. I do not dwell upon it. I wish simply to call it to the reader's attention.

We come now to trace three or four very important things in connection with the beliefs of these people concerning the future. And, in the first place, it is worthy of note that the thought of evolution as connected with death had not entered their minds. They did not regard death as a step in advance. They did not have any forward and upward looking idea or hope connected with it. It was a sad necessity to them. At first there was no ethical idea connected with it. They did not regard it as a punishment; it was only a sad fact that men must die. They did not look forward to it with any anticipation of joy. They pitied those who were obliged to go down into this gloomy and half-unreal world of shades ; and they looked forward to the necessity of it in their own case, as most of us do to-day, as something to be postponed and avoided by every possible means in their power.

I wish to touch on two or three illustrative phases of this belief. There are a good many persons in the modern world who are coming to accept the idea of reincarnation as though it were something desirable, as though it solved the problems and helped them settle some of the practical difficulties of life. Remember, then, that in India, both among the Brahmins and among the Buddhists, it was not a welcome thought. It was held, indeed, almost universally. All men believed that they had existed before, and that they would exist—nobody knew how many times—again. Perhaps in the past they had been kings, or beggars ; they had been diseased and crippled outcasts ; they had been people of wealth and consideration ; they had occupied almost every conceivable position in society. Not only had they been men, perhaps they had been elephants, perhaps they had been apes, perhaps they had been flies or gnats or serpents ; for the kinship of the human and the sub-human was held in India to such an extent that this sort of transformation was not only believed to be possible, but to be actual, and constantly going on. If a man had lived a noble life, he might expect to be born in some higher station after a brief respite in some one of the heavens. If he had lived a bad life, he looked forward to being born in some poorer and meaner condition. And it was not possible for him to balance the good and the bad, to say, " There has been more good in my life than there has been bad," and so have something on his credit account. No matter how good he had been, if he had been bad at all that badness must be expiated to the letter in some rebirth that was to follow.

Dreary, then, was the prospect that awaited them. They could look forward to no rest. There had been thousands, possibly millions, of births in the past ; and there awaited them thousands, perhaps millions, of births in the future. They did not know how many ; and, as they looked forward to it, it seemed an interminable and wearisome round.

The Brahmins and the Buddhists, then, did not anticipate this fate with joy. They did not look forward to it even with resignation ; for the one sole object of the Brahmin religion was to live so as to attain such wisdom as to enable the soul to escape this horrible necessity of being continually reborn. The one thing to look forward to was that he might, after nobody knew how long, attain absorption in Brahma, lose the conciousness of personal identity, forget to think, forget to hope, to desire, to fear, and so share in some impersonal way the felicity of the infinite and eternal spirit.

So this fate was what the Brahmin was trying to escape; and the Buddhist was engaged in the same effort. He had a different philosophy, looked upon the universe in a different way; but he believed also in this eternal, weary round of rebirths. And the one thing that Gautama was striving for was to show his followers the path—to what? The path out of this fearful necessity into Nirvana. And what was Nirvana? Scholars are still disputing over it; but it was either the loss of self-consciousness, the attainment of eternal calm, or else it was something so near unconsciousness that the most careful students find themselves unable to draw any thinkable distinction.

The Brahmins, then, and the Buddhists did not anticipate the next life, except as they looked afar off with an ever-sustained hope to the possibility of losing individual existence and sharing in the supposed impersonal felicity of the Eternal.

The Greeks and the Romans again looked upon this other life, not as something to be desired, but to be dreaded. It was the loss of all they cared for. If you get the picture of it in your minds, you will see how undesirable it must have been. They went down into this underground, shadowy world. They no longer saw the sun, nor the stars at night. They no longer felt the breezes of heaven fanning their brows. They no longer felt the pulsing of the blood in their veins, the free beating of it in their hearts. There was no longer this real, flesh-and-blood existence. There was no longer glad consciousness of power on the part of the athlete, the ability to engage in the struggles of war or the peaceful strifes of the arena. There was no longer the reality of love and friendship such as they had enjoyed in the olden days. It was a shadowy, unreal sort of world where they lived over again in seeming, their memory of what they had cared for in the olden time.

As an illustration of the way it was looked on, let us read over one brief passage from the Odyssey.   Ulysses has been permitted to go down to this underworld ; and he meets there Achilles, the great hero of the ancient world, and in the midst of their conversation he thus addresses him :—

> ".   .   .   .   'But as for thee,
> Achilles, no man lived before thy time,
> Nor will hereafter live, more fortunate
> Than thou,—for while alive we honoured thee
> As if thou wert a god, and now again
> In these abodes thou rulest o'er the dead.
> Therefore, Achilles, shouldst thou not be sad.'
>   I spake.   Achilles, quickly answered me :
> 'Noble Ulysses, speak not thus of death
> As if thou wouldst console me.   I would be
> A labourer on earth, and serve for hire
> Some man of mean estate, who makes scant cheer,
> Rather than reign o'er all who have gone down
> To death.' "

Let us now take one more step, and see that at first there was no ethical idea associated with this fact of death.   By that I mean something twofold.   First, they did not explain the fact of death ethically.   It had no moral significance.   And, in the next place, they had no developed doctrines of rewards or punishments.   Let us consider both of these as briefly as we may and at the same time make them clear.

Men at first took death as a sad fact which they could not avoid; but they did not attempt to explain it in any philosophical way. They did not believe in natural death. They did not see at first why it should be inevitable; and they always held to the belief that, when a man died, it was always because somebody had killed him. But by and by, when they saw that death was universal, they began to see that some general fate hung over them. But they did not regard it as a punishment for anything which they had done. They simply accepted it because they must, without explanation.

Again, it is found that in the early thinking of all these peoples there was in the next world no division between the good and the bad. All went to one place. Death was a sufficient punishment for evil; and it was the same inexplicable thing that also came upon the good. There was no heaven and no hell in the early thinking of these peoples. But by and by, as the moral sense grew, you will see that they inevitably sought some moral explanation of these strange facts. So at last it came about that death was looked upon as a punishment for human sin.

Among the Persians, for example, men were

created with the intention that they should live here on earth for some indefinite period, and then be transferred, without dying, to the abodes of the gods.

There was in the Persian theology one great original Power, and under him two gods in age-long antagonism,—the god of darkness and evil, and the god of good and light,—of apparently equal power. They were matched in an age-long contest; and it was because men took sides with Ahriman, the god of darkness and evil, that they were made, as a punishment, subject to death, which had not been a part of the original creative plan. But in this Persian theology, it is well for us to remember, there were none of the horrors which humanity has imagined in some of these later centuries. There were age-long hells, but all of them were some time to come to an end. Even Ahriman himself, the bad god, and the prototype of the Christian devil, was to be converted and become subject to the deity of light and of good. So that ultimately peace and purity and blessedness were to reign.

In Egyptian theology we find some of the noblest teaching anywhere to be discovered in the world. In the Book of the Dead, which recounts the trial of the soul and its apportionment either to bliss or to misery, there are some of the highest and finest ethical teachings to be found in any religious composition on earth.   The souls are judged with absolute impartiality as to what they are and what they have done, and they go their way into light or darkness as the just assignment of an impartial judge.   But again, in Egypt, the hells are not to last forever.   Punishment was not eternal.

Among the Greeks and Romans death has not been generally explained as the result of any sin on the part of man.   They all at first went down into the underworld.   But, when we come to the highest and finest development of their conceptions of the other life, we find that this underworld is divided into two.   There is Elysium, where the good are as happy as any of the dead can be ; and there is Tartarus, the place where the very wicked are tortured and punished.   But it is worth our careful consideration that generally,—and this, you will see, chimes in remarkably with ordinary Christian dogma,—the bad were punished, not so much because they were bad to their fellow-men, but for some outrage to the gods, some impiety towards them.   They had offended some deity or had profaned some altar, some temple, some sacrifice.

You will see, then, that the growth of ethical ideas concerning the next life keeps pace, and very naturally, with the growth of ethical ideas generally here among men.

There is one other thought now to which I must ask your consideration ; and that is that there came a time, and that, the time of the highest civilisation of these ancient peoples, when scepticism began to come in and invade these hitherto universally accepted beliefs. And there is one principle so important that I must ask you to give it your special attention, —a principle of age-long application, the principle which, in changed conditions and in regard to changed ideas, we are facing to-day.

There is always, at any period of human advance, a great belief, a belief like this that the soul continues after death alive. Then what ? Then there is an intellectual way of stating that belief. There is the formal framework of ideas in which the belief is set. There is the imaginative picture of that other world and of the soul that inhabits it, of its conditions there.

Now, I wish you carefully to separate these two ideas. It is possible for people to hold a belief which is vital and true ; and at the same time it is possible for them to give that belief an intellectual statement which is absurd; so that, as people become wiser and think more carefully about it, they find themselves under the necessity of rejecting it. And then what happens? Why, what is happening right here to-day. The priests, the teachers, the theologians, have so associated the real belief and its intellectual statement as to make them necessary to each other, almost parts of each seem other, practically identical. So when a person finds himself unable any longer to hold the intellectual statement of the belief, he feels that he is losing the belief itself, because he has been taught for ages that the two are inseparably bound together.

Now, the statement which these barbaric peoples had framed of the nature of the soul, the place of its abode, its rewards and punishments was cruel, was ignorant, because it grew up in cruel and ignorant times. But it became consecrated as a part of religion, and the priests did not dare to change it; and it came to be associated in the minds of those who held it with the belief itself. But, as people grew more and more educated, were able to think more clearly and logically, the Olympus, crowned with the gods, became an absurd detail that no sensible man could believe.   The kind of souls that they had talked about they could no longer accept ; and the heavens and the hells came to be questionable, so that the belief in immortality itself began to be questioned,—not by bad people, not by ignorant people,—ignorant and bad people are generally soundly " orthodox" in all ages of the world ; they began to be questioned by the thoughtful and best educated, the best people, because, as I said, intelligence could no longer believe these traditional statements about the gods and the souls and the heavens and the hells.

And so what do we find ? We find, for example, in the noblest period of Roman history, Julius Cæsar, high priest, *Pontifcx Maximus*, the official head of the Roman religion, believing neither in the gods nor in any future life. We find the augurs, men engaged in carrying out the details of the national religion, as it is said, not looking in each other's faces while they were about it, lest they should laugh, because it had come to seem to them unreal and absurd. We find a writer like Lucian—almost, perhaps, an ancient duplicate of Colonel Ingersoll to-day. He was witty, gifted with a power of satire and ridicule that has rarely been matched, and, as we would say, poking infinite fun at the whole universe—ridiculing the gods, ridiculing the other life, all the popular beliefs of his time, and making them so ridiculous that any person who carefully thought would find it impossible to hold them in those old ways any longer.

So this inevitable period of scepticism came. And it will come in every age inevitably, so long as the priests and the leaders in the religious life insist upon creating fictitious infallibilities. Fit out any set of ideas with the attribute of infallibility, and, when they are outgrown, you will have an inevitable period of scepticism. The only way to escape it is to keep thought free, so that, while people cherish the inner and central faith of their religion, the form may take infinite liberty in changing and adapting itself to the intellectual conditions of the time.

Socrates, Plato, Plutarch, Cicero, Seneca, and their fellows speculated, talked, and wrote about these great questions very much as thoughtful men have been doing ever since their time. They believed or they doubted and tried to believe. They hoped and they sought and attempted to give consolation in face of the inevitable fate. To-day we find their arguments strong or weak, according as the trend of our own thinking leads. They witness, at any rate, to the inextinguishable thirst of the human soul for an answer to its eternal question.

There swept, then, over the ancient world a great wave of doubt as to the reality of any future life ; but I want you to note carefully that this doubt did not necessarily touch the innermost heart of the belief, only its outward form, its statement. And I wish you to note, further, that these intellectual discussions did not disturb or upset the great deep-down faiths of the common people. These waited for some period when there should be a larger and clearer conception that should clothe these old trusts, and make them once more acceptable to the philosophers, the scientists, and the scholars of the time.

THE OLD TESTAMENT AND
IMMORTALITY

I PROPOSE in this chapter to outline as clearly and simply as I can the growth and changes of belief among the Hebrew people. You will understand that this belief changes, that there are all phases of it from the beginning to the end, and that it is impossible to sum it up in any one general phrase. I shall then outline, in simple, plain fashion, the growth and changes of this faith. A topic like this does not admit of enthusiastic treatment. I cannot, while dealing legitimately and fairly, play upon your passions and your feelings, rouse you to high pitches of excitement. I must rather keep along the commonplace level of simple narrative and description. But this characteristic of my theme will not hold true of a good many others that are to follow.

There is one very striking thing at the outset. Tradition tells us that Moses, having been discovered hidden away in the bulrushes on the banks of the Nile, was adopted by the daughter of Pharaoh, and treated and trained as her son. And we are told that he was learned in all the wisdom of the Egyptians. If this tradition be reliable, of course he must have had an intimate and comprehensive acquaintance with the ordinary Egyptian beliefs about this world, about the gods, about the other life. And yet Moses is the founder, not only of the religion, but of the Jewish state. He is the one who, as tradition tells us, gave shape at the outset to the young Hebrew civilisation.

Now, if there is any one thing that is apparent on the face of Egyptian belief, it is that they held the strongest kind of imaginative belief in another life. It is said that the young Egyptian, almost before he made preparations for keeping house in this world, began to make preparations for his tomb, looking forward to his relation to that life which was to follow this. Perhaps there is no other nation in antiquity in which this belief in another life was more clearly and universally accepted and developed. And yet here we face the striking fact that I referred to a moment ago. When

Moses comes to give shape to the Hebrew state and religion, he takes absolutely no account whatever of any belief in any other life than this.   There is nowhere in that part of the Bible which is especially associated with Moses any clear teaching of any future life at all.   There is nowhere any doctrine as to rewards in another life for good deeds in this, or of punishment in any other life for bad deeds in this.   The other life, in other words, plays no part in the Mosaic tradition.

How shall we account for this?   There have been a great many explanations offered. Some have suggested that Moses came to think that the Egyptians laid too much emphasis on the other life, to the neglect of this one, and that, therefore, he left it practically out of account in his legislation.   Others have said that, by a natural feeling of revulsion, the escaped slaves would be sure to hate whatever was associated with their former oppressors and masters.   And yet there are certain very striking characteristics of the Hebrew religion which have their counterparts and parallels in the Egyptian.   I am not ready to say that Moses borrowed them from the Egyptians, but it looks on the surface very much like it.   The one central feature, almost, of the Jewish religion is the ark. The ark was one of the principal features of the Egyptian religion. Among the early Hebrews Yahweh, the national god, was worshipped in the figure of a bull. This was one of the commonest of the Egyptian idols; and the significance attached to it by the two peoples was substantially the same. So it does not seem to me that we can find right here the explanation for the strange fact that Moses should have left the other life so entirely out of account. Perhaps it is not worth our while to spend much time in trying to explain it. The fact is there, and it is worthy of our notice; and perhaps that is enough for our purpose.

Now, I wish in a general way to emphasise what I have said in regard to the so-called Mosaic legislation, and state a few common facts concerning the whole Old Testament. The word "heaven" and the word "hell" appear very frequently, indeed, in the Old Testament; and, when I was reading these chapters, as a boy, I naïvely took it for granted that the writers were talking about the same kind of heaven and hell that I had been trained to believe in. But I wish you to note with a great deal of care that there is not one single place throughout the whole Old Testament where the word "heaven" means what we are accustomed to associate with that name as popularly used to-day. There is not one place in the whole Old Testament where the word "hell" means what we mean by it to-day. So there is no doctrine of heaven and hell, in the modern theological sense, in the whole Old Testament.

There is not a case where anybody ever goes to hell in the Old Testament as the result of his bad deeds. There are only two cases in the whole Old Testament where anybody ever goes to heaven; and those two find their basis chiefly in tradition rather than anything else. Those two cases you will readily remember: they are Enoch and Elijah. It is said of Enoch, "And Enoch walked with God; and he was not, for God took him." This is all that the narrative says. But the belief grew up in after times that what this really meant was that God had taken Enoch directly to heaven without his passing through the process of dying.

The other case is the familiar story of Elijah. In his old age he is walking with his companion prophet, Elisha; and suddenly there appear horses of fire and chariots of fire, and, before the astonished eyes of his compatriot, Elijah is seized away from his presence and caught up by a whirlwind into heaven. This is the record of the other supposed translation.

You will note that neither is especially clear on the subject ; but they are distinguished as being the only two cases in the Old Testament where anybody is supposed to have gone to heaven.

Now, in order that I may make perfectly clear the teaching of the Old Testament concerning death and another life, I wish to quote and comment on a few of the principal passages in the Old Testament that are supposed to have some bearing on some phase of this problem. And, in the first place, take the passage that tells us about the creation of Adam,—" And the Lord God formed man of the dust of the ground, and breathed into his nostrils the breath of life ; and man became a living soul."

A great many persons are accustomed to suppose that this teaches by implication the fact of the immortal life, because, if man became the possessor of a living soul, that, they think, would go on. But the moment we look beneath the surface, and see that the word translated " soul " is precisely the same word which in other parts of the Old Testament is used to denote the life principle of animals, we see that it either proves too little or too much. Undoubtedly, the writer of that passage did not have this thought in his mind one way or the other.

I have said there was no clear doctrine of another life in the Old Testament; and yet we find cropping up in the lives of the common people a belief which at least takes us a little way across the border, and suggests that thoughts in this direction were beginning to come into the popular mind. Take the command in Exodus,—" Thou shalt not suffer a witch to live." In Deuteronomy there is legislation concerning divination and witchcraft. Then there is that famous story—the best example of all—of the witch of Endor, and how, to please Saul, she calls up the spirit of the old prophet Samuel.

But, if we study the characteristics of the real belief of the people at that time, we shall find,—what I shall emphasise in a moment,— that this spirit of Samuel was supposed to have been in a sort of comatose, unconscious condition, either connected with the place where he was buried or in that crude and indefinite underworld which was the first stage

in the growth of sheol.   He is disturbed and
roused by the witch's magic out of this sleep,
this condition of unconsciousness, utters his
message, and goes back into that condition
again.

Undoubtedly, here is the beginning of the
belief in an underworld ; but it is anything but
clear, and it was frowned upon by the authorities, the representatives of the priesthood.
It was made a crime to have thus any communion with the dead.

It is worth our taking careful note of, right
here, that among the Hebrew people, as you
will find at all stages of their career, there was
a belief in the possibility of communication
between the two worlds.   We find that a similar thing has been true in every nation, in
every religion that we are able to investigate.

I am taking these passages, not certainly in
chronological order, but in the order of the
books as they stand in our Bible now.   I wish
you to note the picture of this other life as it
appears in Job—if you can call it life.   He says,
" Before I go whence I shall not return, even
to the land of darkness and the shadow of
death : a land of darkness, as darkness itself ;
and of the shadow of death, without any
order, and where the light is as darkness."

This is his picture,—the picture of the condition of the shades as it had developed itself up to the time of Job. The soul did not go quite into extinction ; but it went down into this shadowy, underground world, where there was no real life, no consciousness, where it was close on the borders of annihilation.

But there is another passage in Job which has been made a great deal of, which seems to take a long step forward. You remember it, —" For I know that my Redeemer liveth, and that He shall stand at the latter day upon the earth." It is unfortunate that this word " Redeemer" should be here in this passage ; and it is not here in the Revised Version. Every scholar knows that it has no sort of connection with the thought of a Redeemer, as we are accustomed to use that word. Job has been accused, and, he feels, unjustly accused ; and he simply stoutly asserts his belief that his vindicator liveth and that this vindicator will some time appear for his deliverance and justify his contention that he is innocent. So you see this has no real bearing on this subject at all.

Here is a little passage from the Psalms that does seem to have a very strong implication in that connection. Unfortunately, we are not able, with any definiteness, to assign the time when these particular passages were written. If we could, we might get a very much clearer idea of the order of growth of belief among the Hebrew people. The writer of this Psalm—we have no idea who he was—says, " Thou wilt not leave my soul in hell [sheol], neither wilt thou suffer thine holy one to see corruption." Here is the beginning of that dawn of hope of deliverance from this underworld to which I shall call your attention in a moment.

The ordinary tone of the Psalmists concerning death is not at all hopeful. Take this one. He is asking God to keep him alive, and let him offer Him acceptable worship while he is here. He says :

" What profit is there in my blood when I go down to the pit ? Shall the dust praise thee ? Shall it declare thy truth ? Wilt thou show wonders to the dead ? Shall the dead arise and praise thee ? Shall thy loving-kindness be declared in the courts or thy faithfulness in destruction ? Shall thy wonders be known in the dark, or thy truth in the land of forgetfulness ? "

And then the writer of Ecclesiastes :

" For there is no remembrance of the wise more than the fool forever,—seeing that which now is, in the days to come shall all be forgotten. And how dieth the wise man ? As the fool ? " " For the living know that they shall die ; but the dead know not anything, neither have they any more reward, for the memory of them is forgotten."

And then that famous passage towards the end of the book : "Whatsoever thy hand findeth to do, do it with thy might ; for there is no work, nor device, nor knowledge, nor wisdom, in the grave whither thou goest."

In another place is a touch of the Oriental doctrine of reabsorption into Deity. It is not to be personal immortality at all. "Then shall the dust return to the earth as it was, and the spirit shall return unto God who gave it." The person is made up of two elements, the finer spiritual side and the earthly; and they go back, and are reabsorbed into whence they came.

Now, there is one very striking picture of the condition of belief in this underworld to be found in Isaiah. The prophet is addressing the King of Babylon, and foretelling what is coming to him. He says :

" Hell from beneath is moved for thee to meet thee at thy coming ; it stirreth up the dead for thee, even all the chief ones of the earth ; it hath raised up from their thrones all the kings of the nations. And they shall speak, and say unto thee, Art thou also become weak as we ? art thou become like unto us ? Thy pomp is brought down to the grave, and the noise of thy viols ; the worm is spread under thee, and the worms cover thee."

This in Isaiah is a picture of what was expected in the future.

There is a very famous passage in Daniel. Daniel, you must remember, however, was written within two hundred years of the time of Christ ; and beyond question it represents the dawning of a great and hopeful belief, to which I shall call your attention in a moment. " Many of them that sleep in the dust of the earth shall awake, some to everlasting life, and some to shame and everlasting contempt."

These extracts give you a fair and fairly adequate conception of the Old Testament teaching concerning belief in another life, if you call it life.   Now I wish to go back, and indicate to you in broad outline some of the steps of the growth of this belief.

The Hebrew people in their religious thought and practice ranged all the way from the lowest barbarism up to the highest period of their civilisation in the time of Jesus.   At the outset they were nature-worshippers.   They were sex-worshippers, with rites which to-day would seem to us obscene.   They were sacrificers of human beings, even their own children ; and, at the time when we find them in this condition, there is no belief in any desirable future life at all. At first there begins, just as we find it among all barbaric peoples, the notion that a shade may haunt the place of burial; and this grave at lasts develops into the thought of an underground abode, and this expands and grows larger as the thought of the people changes and expands.

At first, then, we must remember, that the Hebrew universe was a very small affair. Think, for example,—heaven, as their early writers pictured it, this blue dome above us, the " firmament," as it was called, was like a brass dome or cover, beaten out and shut down around the edge of the earth,—I do not know how to explain it better than to say like the cover of a dinner platter. It was regarded as solid. There were little windows in it to let the rain through. Up above this were stored the waters above the firmament, in contrast with the seas and lakes and rivers, the waters beneath the firmament. There was no underground world there. But above this firmament was heaven, where God and His angels abode; but no people went there, no human beings dreamed of such a thing as looking forward to that kind of destiny.

Throughout the Old Testament, if you will

note it carefully as you read, there is no ethical significance attached to the life after death. There is no future punishment for sin at first, indeed almost nowhere in the Old Testament. It is the inevitable fate of men ; but the good and the bad all alike go down into this under-world, one destiny awaits them all, and one hopelessness hangs with its gloom over them all. The only punishment that is ever threatened in the greater part of the Old Testament for flagrant wrong-doing is that men shall die. The one great reward held out for goodness is health, long life, many children, wealth, consideration among one's people, friends, and fame,—all rewards attaching to this life.

But of necessity an ethical sense must spring up among the Jews, because it springs up among all peoples after they reach a certain stage of development. The Book of Job concerns itself with the problem that sprang out of this old and popular idea. It was found that good people did not necessarily have better health than bad people. It was found that good people did not live seventy or eighty years, any more surely than bad people. It was found that the good were not always rich, not always prosperous, that they were not always blessed with children, that they were not always famous among their people ; and it was found that bad people as frequently carried off the rewards of this life as did the virtuous. Thus they found that this theory would not work. Then there sprang up in their belief, as there has all over the world out of a similar experience, the belief in some future life of rewards and punishments, where the inequalities of the present should be readjusted. This seemed to them a fundamental demand of justice. If God were righteous, there must be a reward for goodness. If God were righteous, there must be punishment sometime and somewhere for wrong ; and, if it did not appear in this world, then it must appear in some other world.

So, out of reasoning like this, and the natural development of this first thin shade and the hollow connected with the grave, there grew at last the great underworld, which they called "sheol," mistranslated hell: or, rather, let me say, it is translated well ; for hell comes from the same root as "hole," and originally meant only an underground cavern. In progress of time and change of thought it was narrowed at last and limited to a place of punishment, but that was not its original meaning. So in the prayer-book, where it says that Christ descended into hell, it does not necessarily mean that he went to a place of torment.

There grew up, then, in the course of Jewish progress of thought a belief in the underworld ; but the life down there was no more desirable than we find it to have been among the Greeks and the Romans. It was giving up the bright sunlight and the beauty and glory of this world under the sun and stars, and going down into a world of shadows. It was a fate from which to escape, if possible ; and so, naturally, there grew in the minds of the people a belief that the good, at any rate, who were imprisoned in sheol, should escape.

This led to the doctrine of the resurrection. I shall have occasion to point out to you a very important distinction. The doctrine of the resurrection does not necessarily mean the resurrection of the body : it means a re-surrection,—that is, a coming up again after having gone down somewhere. That is what the word means. So the Jews came to believe that those who were imprisoned in sheol could come up again, be resurrected. Whether they were joined to their old bodies or not was entirely another question, to be settled by other considerations.

So the doctrine came to be taught,—which

was that these people imprisoned in the underworld should by and by be set free, and come up into the light again; and when was this to be? You see we are a long distance from any heaven yet. This was to be at the time of the coming of the Messiah. The Messiah was to appear, represent God's justice towards His own people and His judgment on their enemies, and sit enthroned on Mount Moriah; the trumpet was to be blown and the dead were to come up from sheol, from this underworld; those who had been good, and faithful in the past, who had believed Him and served God according to the light they possessed, and looked forward with hope to deliverance in the future,—these were to rise first; and they were to reign with the Messiah on the earth for a thousand years.

This was the magnificent belief that at last sprang up from the instincts and longings of the Hebrew heart. Some of the people believed that they were to be joined to their bodies, and some did not; some believed that the good and bad both were to be raised out of sheol; some believed that only the good were to be raised. You see there were all varieties of speculation, just as there are to-day, and just as there will be so long as human nature is what we know it to be now. Some believed that the bad, when they were raised, were to be cast into severe and age-long punishment. Others believed that they were to be destroyed,—in what is called to-day "Conditional Immortality."

Now, what kind of a world was this underworld ? I have said that nobody went to heaven ; and yet the belief grew up that the good were rewarded in this underworld and the bad were punished. What accommodation, then, was made for the inhabitants of sheol ? There was a dividing line,—that line which the Hebrew writers tell us was not thicker than a thread ; but it separated as by a great gulf Gehenna and Paradise. All the dead went down into sheol, or hades ; the good went to Paradise, and the bad went to Gehenna. But they were so near together that they could see from one place across to the other, and even converse with each other, as appears in some of the parables of Jesus.

You will notice that I have gone a good way beyond the letter of the Old Testament. I have included in my discussion the growth of this belief in the other life up to the time of Jesus, across the great gulf of two or three hundred years represented by the blank leaves

between the Testaments. Though most people do not take the trouble to familiarise themselves with what was going on during that
time, those who have studied it know that it
was one of the most intensely active and
creative epochs in the history of the Jewish
people.

There grew up the belief that God had intended that men should be immortal here on
earth ; that nobody should ever die ; that it was
only sin that led to death ; that, if they had
been obedient, they would have lived here
until they were translated, without any death.
A large part of the belief which I have outlined, you note, covers this period of the blank
between the Testaments ; but this development of the doctrine of the underworld, of
Paradise and Gehenna, both in Sheol, or
Hades, did not appear in the letter of the Old
Testament at all, but was one of the later
growths of the Hebrew faith.

At the time when Jesus was born we find
three phases of belief which are worthy of our
attention.

First there were the Sadducees. I think the
popular idea is that the Sadducees were a sort
of modern sceptics of their time. So far from
that 's being the truth, the Sadducees were the

old, staid, respectable, "mossback" conservatives : they were the ones who claimed to stand
by the letter of the Mosaic law ; and, therefore,
they believed neither in angel nor spirit, and
had no belief in any future life at all. They
were the old conservatives. They represented
the old-time Mosaic tradition.

Then there were the Essenes. They were
a sort of philosophical Platonists. They believed in a future life, but not in the resurrection of the body. They believed that the
spirit was imprisoned here for a time in the
body ; but, by and by, through death, it escaped, and entered into the place prepared
for it.

But the great popular party among the
Jews—those that represented their grandest
traditions, patriotic and religious as well—
were the Pharisees. And the Pharisees held
that the traditions of the elders were of equal
authority with the old-time Mosaic teaching ;
and they had borrowed from the Babylonians
or Persians the whole angelic hierarchy and of
evil spirits as well, so that popularly they held
not only a belief in immortality, but in innumerable evil spirits and innumerable good
spirits. A man was surrounded by thousands
of them, one class attempting to lead him to

good and the other influencing him towards evil, so that he lived and walked every day in the midst of innumerable invisible inhabitants of the other world. This was the general Pharisaic belief at that time. So common did they believe these spirits to be that it is said that a man, if he threw a stone over his shoulder, or threw away from himself a broken piece of pottery, asked pardon of any spirit that he might possibly have hit in so doing. This was the kind of world that was believed in by the Pharisees at the time Jesus was born.

We see, then, as the summed up result of this brief outline that, although there was no teaching apparent and emphasised on the surface of the Old Testament, there really was a common belief underneath the surface, growing up in the hearts and imaginations of the common people; and we see also what we commonly misunderstand, that these other worlds took the shape which they had to take. Sometimes, as we look back and are studying the conditions of thought in the past, we are moved, perhaps, with feelings of scorn or contempt, and wonder how anybody could have held such ideas. But the evolutionist who studies carefully the growth of human thought, who traces it step by step, knows that at every stage of human progress men have been as rational as their brain development at the time permitted them to be. They have reasoned as well as we reason to-day, in accordance with the facts with which they were familiar or what they supposed to be facts.

Thus the intellectual picture of this other life, its location, its inhabitants, its activities, was the background, or framework, that the intellectual development of the time was capable of outlining.

The moral idea, the thought of rewards and punishments, was the best that the moral development of the time was capable of framing; and the spiritual ideas and spiritual hopes were foregleams and foreshadows of the higher and finer and nobler truths of which we are gaining glimpses to-day. ·

So the Hebrews, in common with all the other great peoples of the past, were passing through their normal and necessary stage of evolution in regard to this matter, their thought leading on to that which doth not yet appear.

IV

PAUL'S DOCTRINE OF DEATH AND THE OTHER LIFE

PAUL says in the first chapter of the Epistle to the Philippians, the twenty-third and twenty-fourth verses, " For I am in a strait betwixt two, having a desire to depart and to be with Christ; which is far better. Nevertheless to abide in the flesh is more needful for you."

This, you note, is Paul's general view of life and death. Unselfishly, he is willing to abide with the disciples, with those who are anxious to learn the new truth and to carry on his work. He recognises that it is better that he should do it; but note the significance of his feeling, and the strangeness of that significance,—if he could have his own way, he would choose to die. Have there been many companions of Paul in that choice, in the history of the world? He really believed that to depart, and be with Christ, was a good deal better than anything he could find here.

I have chosen to take up the belief and teaching of Paul before that of Jesus, for the reason that the record of his belief precedes the record of the belief of Jesus. That is, in the chronological order in which the books were written, the Epistles of Paul come earlier than the Gospels. I am following the chronological order of the record, then, rather than the chronological order of the teaching itself; and I do it for the reason that it is possible that the beliefs put upon the lips of the Master may have been coloured by the opinions of the time when the record was made, so there may be a step onward to be observed in the Gospels beyond that which we find in the acknowledged Epistles of Paul.

So much merely by way of introduction and explanation.

We have observed up to the present time, in our study of the history of belief in immortality, that the people of the old world, before Christianity, almost universally held this belief. The exceptions have been so few as to be hardly worthy of our notice. The belief in some sort of continued existence after the fact we call death was practically universal from the beginning of human thought down to the birth of Christ. But note another point in connection with that. Death has not been regarded as anything desirable. It has been looked upon as a calamity. Going into the other world was not thought to be an ascent; it was descent. The next life was poorer than this, not richer. The men who went down into the shades left behind them the pulsing, breathing life of the flesh. They became thin shadows. They left the blessed light of the sun, the fair blue heaven overhead. They left the green earth, the waving trees, the music of the brooks and of the waves upon the shore. They left the life of ambition, the fierce joy of strife and battle, the aims and hopes of future advance, all the joys of home, of companionship, of husband and wife, of children. They left all that made life seem sweetest and best, and went down into an underworld of shades.

They lived, to be sure; but it was only a kind of half-life, and, as I have said, not at all to be desired. But, as in the early twilight we hear a note in this direction, and another in that, of some half-wakened bird, that precludes and prophesies the outburst of song that shall accompany the dawn, so here and there, throughout the ancient world, we come upon a note now and then—from India, Persia, China—of hope, of cheer; someone daring to believe that death is not so great a calamity after all. But, for the most part, it is either a sort of stoic resignation, facing the inevitable and trying to believe that the inevitable must be somehow bearable, or else it is an utter succumbing to a fear of the shadow which cannot be escaped. The condition of the world may fairly be represented by those words of the New Testament where it speaks of men as "through fear of death all their lifetime subject to bondage."

I wish to give you one splendid illustration of pre-Christian thought and dawning hope in regard to this matter of death. The noblest character—I suppose all of us are agreed—to be found in the ancient world is perhaps that of Socrates; and there is no man who has spoken, if he be correctly represented by Plato, more sweetly, hopefully, grandly, in regard to death, than he. I wish to give you a specimen of that beginning of trust, voiced by Socrates, to be found in the pre-Christian world:

" Those of us who think that death is an evil are in error. There is great reason to hope that death is a good." You see, he does not feel sure about it. " For one of two things,—either death is a state of nothingness and utter unconsciousness, or there is a migration of the soul from this world to another.

" Now, if there is no consciousness, but a sleep undisturbed by dreams, death will be a gain ; for eternity is
then but a single night.

" But if death is the journey to another place, and
there all the dead are, what good, O my friends, can be
greater than this ? What would not a man give if he
might converse with Orpheus and Musæus and Hesiod
and Homer? Nay, if this be true, let me die again and
again. I shall have a wonderful interest in there meeting and conversing with the heroes of old.

" Above all, I shall then be able to continue my
search into knowledge. What delight would there be in
conversing with (the great and good) and asking them
questions.

" (And) besides being happier in that world than in
this, they will be immortal, if what is said is true.

" Wherefore, be of good cheer about death, and know
of a certainty that no evil can happen to a good man
either in life or after death. To die and be released (is)
better for me."

See what a striking forecast that is to the
words of Paul, which I have taken as a text.

" I am not angry with my condemners or
with my accusers. They have done me no
harm, although they did not intend to do me
any good; and for this I may gently blame
them."

This, you know, is related as being what he
said to his judges when about to drink the
hemlock :

" The hour of departure has arrived ; and

we go our ways,—I to die, and you to live. Which is better God only knows."

This is the magnificent utterance, the wonderful attitude, of the old Greek.

But a new note is sounded with the coming of the Christian hope. In Paul's words there is no question : To die or to live, which is better God only knows. He has no question about it. And it is no stoic indifference with which he faces the fact of death. He defies Death, smiles in his face, clasps his hand as a friend, and looks forward eagerly to the time when he will be free from his duties and obligations here, and be permitted to take him by the hand and be led out into that larger and grander life. This is the attitude of Paul. "To die is gain," he says in another place ; and in another : "O death, where is thy sting? O grave, where is thy victory? Thanks be to God which giveth us the victory through our Lord Jesus Christ." Paul, then, was looking forward to death as the gateway to the all-desired, the consummation of his highest and most brilliant hope.

It will be interesting for us now, I think, to note the general scheme of the world and of the universe, as Paul held it, how he came to hold these views, and just what they meant at his time.   We shall see, as we go on, that they meant something very different from what they mean in the ordinary use that we make of them to-day, or as interpreted in the creeds of the churches.

What does Paul hold?   He does not make much of it; but, incidentally, we are perfectly certain that Paul thinks that before the creation of the earth there had been a rebellion in heaven.   On a certain date, at a specified time, Christ had been set forth, proclaimed the special Son and representative of God, appointed the leader of the angels.   And then Lucifer,—otherwise called Satan, the Devil,— through envy on account of thwarted ambition, having hoped to fill this position himself, rebels against God and the heavenly order, and leads a third part of the angels, who follow him in this rebellion; and he is cast out of heaven.   The blessed felicity of that place is no longer to be disturbed by discord; and so he is hurled down to the abyss, to the home, the place prepared for him.   But meanwhile he occupies a position between the heavens above and the earth beneath; that is, he is released from his imprisonment, is able to escape for the time, that he may tempt and work his will, so far as they submit to it, upon the men and women living here upon the earth. So the New Testament doctrine, generally, and the doctrine of Paul is, that Satan, Lucifer, the Devil, is "the Prince of the Power of the Air." There is a kingdom of evil spirits in the atmosphere about us, between the earth and the sky.

This is the general idea which Paul held in regard to the rebellion in heaven and the kingdom of evil which the Devil set up in his attempt to thwart the purposes of God in the creation of this world. After this rebellion in heaven the world is created, the Garden eastward in Eden. You know the story,—how man is tempted by this would-be leader of the hosts of heaven who still continues his warfare against God and His Christ and all good, and how he fell as the result of this temptation. And with this fall the apostle teaches that death, hitherto unknown in any world or any epoch, comes upon men. Death enters by the doorway which sin has opened. It is God's penalty for the evil which men have wrought.

It would appear that Paul believed what we know to have been a common opinion of his time; that, if there had been no sin, men would have lived, either forever here on this earth (as they could hardly have held if they had thought a little deeply about the matter), or that, after they had lived an indefinite time here, they would be translated, perhaps transformed and spiritualised into another kind of being, and permitted to enter into the presence of God in the heavens above. This was to have been the course, if there had been no sin; but sin came, and then " death passed upon all men," to use the words of Paul, " for that all had sinned."

Now what became of these persons who were thus subjects of death? Where were they? They were in the underworld. We must understand clearly if we wish to get the idea of Paul and make it real to us, what kind of universe it was in which he lived. Paul's universe was a sort of three-story affair : there was this earth, the dome of blue above, and beyond that a little way was heaven, where God had His celestial court ; but no men were there. Not a man from the foundation of the world— with the possible exception of Enoch and Elijah—had ever entered the presence of God in heaven. And then, underneath the surface of this flat earth, the underworld, as approachable as any island of the sea, if only a person could find out the way,—the underworld of the dead, a cavern, Sheol, Hades ; and all the dead, good and bad together, went down into this underworld. It was some thousands of years before the idea of separating this underworld into two parts entered the minds of the Hebrews. But by the time of Paul there was a place of suffering, called Gehenna, —that is the Greek form for the Valley of Hinnom, this being a place where the refuse of the city was cast out to be burned; and so this is used as the figure of moral and spiritual refuse, the place of destruction. And on the other hand was Paradise, a place where the good souls waited until the end of their captivity should come.

All, then, the good and the bad, were held captive by death and shut up in this underworld. When were they to be released, and how, according to the belief of Paul? It was the belief of the Hebrews in the later part of their history that at the coming of the Messiah all the Jews, at any rate all those who had believed in the Messiah and had waited for him, were to be raised up from this underworld, reclothed with their bodies and become subjects of the Messianic kingdom, permitted to live here in the glory of that time which they had seen in dream and hope far away, and which they had done their share in preparing for.

This was the general belief of the Hebrews. Paul, of course, shared this belief. We must remember that he was a Pharisee ; and, if there is any point in his creed concerning which we are in darkness, we shall be safe in supposing that he held the ordinary, Pharisaic doctrine relating to it.

But a change came over the faith of Paul. He accepted at last the idea that Jesus was the Messiah the Jews had been so long looking for. But, at the advent, Jesus came when they were not expecting him. He came, too, as a feeble child : he grew up unknown ; and nothing strange had happened there at the time of his advent,—no resurrection of the dead, good or bad,—and he lived to be thirty years old before anybody found out that he was the Messiah. Then, as Paul believed, he was revealed to the inner few as the expected Christ. Paul believed that he was the Christ ; for, as you read his Epistles, you will notice that one of the great points in his preaching everywhere was his attempt to convince his Hebrew hearers that Jesus was the Christ, the Messiah.

Nothing happened, then, at the advent. So far the general expectation of the Hebrews was disappointed. Now what change took place in their faith ?   A belief arose in a second advent.   Jesus had been a different kind of Messiah from what they had expected : he had come to suffer and to die instead of to reign. But at last they came to hold that this was an atonement for sin, in order to break down and do away with the old Mosaic law, and that after his death (his atoning death of sacrifice) he was to come again.   A second advent was looked for ; and at this second advent all the wonderful things were to happen which had been expected at the time of his first coming, on the part of the ordinary Jews.

Now what did Paul believe was to happen ? First let me answer a preliminary question : When did Paul expect this second advent to take place?   It is very curious to see how people turn and torture and twist Scripture to bring it into accordance with their preconceived ideas ; but, if there is any one thing that is absolutely certain, it is that Paul and all the apostles and the early disciples, and the early churches generally, believed that Jesus was to come in the clouds of heaven to put an end to this present world dispensation, and to usher in the next epoch, and that he was to do it immediately—that is, at least within the generation then living.   They preached that

he might come at any time. They were to
look for him as a thief comes in the night, un-
expectedly ; they were to watch ; they were to
be ready. " In such an hour as ye think not
the Son of man cometh " : as lightning shineth
from one part of heaven to another, so the
coming of the Son of man shall be. Paul
talked as though this were to be immediately.
All the disciples so talked. The New Testament is on tiptoe of expectation.

What did Paul expect to happen when he
did come ? He expected that the world would
be roused by the sound of the archangel's
trump ringing from one end of heaven to the
other, startling those that were not ready, not
expecting it, and thrilling with joy those who
had waited and were prepared. And what
was to happen ? At the sound of that trump
the dull ears of those that were in Hades were
to become attentive and listen. The dead in
Christ, those who had died believing and hop-
ing in Christ, were to rise first. There is a
curious illustration of the reality and vividness
of this belief to be found in the Epistles to the
Thessalonians. Evidently, the Thessalonian
people had expected that all the believers were
going to live until this second advent was made
manifest. And they were disturbed when one

after another died; and they wrote to Paul and said : " What does this mean ?   Are these persons that have suffered, been persecuted, and been waiting for the coming of Christ, to die, after all, and not see the glory in which they have believed ?"   Then Paul writes them a comforting word.   You will find it in the Second Epistle to the Thessalonians.   He says : Do not be disturbed.   Do not expect the coming too suddenly.   There is to be a revelation of evil breaking loose and accomplishing certain things before that coming. But the point for your consolation is this : those that are alive are not to prevent (*prevenio*, the word meaning to come before) those that are asleep ; that is, those of us who are alive when Christ comes are not to be any better off than those who have died, because at the sound of that trump those who have believed and waited for Christ are suddenly to rise, and we who are alive are to be changed in a moment, "in the twinkling of an eye." We are not to die ; but we are to pass through this miraculous transformation—put off our present bodies, be clothed with our spiritual bodies, join those who are raised from the dead, and meet the Lord in the air.   This is Paul's comfort to the Thessalonians, who wondered if they were going to lose anything by being dead before this marvellous advent took place.

Now, I wish you to note what is of prime importance,—the significance of the fact of resurrection. Jesus was to do two things by his life, sufferings, and death, and his rising again from the dead. In the first place, he was to abolish the law. It had been found by trial that the law did not make people good: it only revealed to them their wickedness, their evil. They were unconscious of it without the law; but the law, holding up its strict claim showed them what failures they were. So Paul said it was impossible to be saved by the law, because no one could keep it. The only hope was in the abolition of the law and the setting up of a kingdom of grace. The law made a terrible mistake when it put to death a perfect being. It abrogated itself by so doing, and became thenceforth a dead letter. So Christ abolished the law. The next thing he did was to bring life and immortality to light. This is according to the opinion of Paul. Paul does not care anything about the physical resurrection of Jesus from the tomb of Joseph of Arimathea. When he speaks of those who had seen the risen Jesus,

he classes himself among them, although he
distinctly says he never saw Jesus in the flesh.
He saw him in a vision on the road to Damascus,—saw him, as he claimed, in his spiritual
body. This is what Paul meant by seeing
Jesus.

But the thing that Paul insisted on was that
Jesus was alive, and not dead; that he had
escaped from sheol, or hades, and ascended
into heaven; that he had broken the bonds of
death through the power of the Father, so
that death could no longer hold him; and he
had demonstrated the power of life by becoming—what? The "first-fruits of them that
sleep." In other words, note, Paul says that
Jesus, or the Christ, was the first one from the
foundation of the world who ever escaped from
the prison-house of death, underground, and
ascended into heaven. He was the first-fruits
from the dead.

I wish you to note here that Paul is a Unitarian. Paul is not the kind of Unitarian that
is known to-day. He is what we should call to-
day, conforming to theological distinctions, an
Arian. He believed in the pre-existence of
Christ, that he had lived in heaven. But he
distinctly says of him that he was the first-
born among the creatures, "the first-born

of every creature " not the Creator ; not the
original, primal God.   He is the first-born of
the creatures in his advent, the first-born from
the dead in his resurrection, which demon-
strates that men can be raised from the dead.

And now, as illustrating Paul's belief concerning the Christ, and his general belief,
let me call your attention to this important
chapter, the famous fifteenth chapter of First
Corinthians.   I wonder that the people who
believe in the literal resurrection of the body
should not have noted the teaching of Paul,
or, noticing it, should have paid no attention
to it.   Paul distinctly and definitely says that
the body that is to be raised is not the body
that was buried.   He says : You plant a grain
of wheat.   That which is raised is not that
grain of wheat : there is some connection between that and the new life ; but this is only a
bare grain.   God raises that grain of wheat
into a glorious body, infinitely finer and fairer
than that which is buried ; but it is another
body such as it pleases God to give.   So he
says ; In the resurrection of the dead that body
which is buried in the grave is not to be raised.

And I wish you to note now—for I cannot
lay too much emphasis on it, it has been so
many years utterly forgotten or misunderstood

or misinterpreted—that the resurrection in the New Testament means always the resurrection from this underworld, the coming up again out of hades, or sheol, the world of shadow, the prison-house of the dead. It does not mean the raising up of the body; and it does not mean what we are apt to interpret it as meaning to-day, the mere rising of the soul in the moment of death. Paul did not believe that the soul was raised at the moment of death : he believed that it went to hades, this prison-house of the dead ; but the resurrection means, literally, a rising again,—not an ascent, not a coming up, but a rising again after going down, the rising up from sheol, or hades, of those who have descended there at the moment of death.

This is the resurrection which Paul teaches ; and it is this resurrection—the significance of which lies in the fact that the power of death is broken — that he preaches in regard to Christ. He tells us that, when Christ escaped from hades and ascended on high, he led with him a multitude of captives accompanying his ascent, the first-fruits of those who had been in sheol for so long. The significance, then, of the resurrection according to Paul was that the power of death had been broken; and henceforth men were delivered from that power.

I wish now to raise the question for a moment as to whether Paul gives us material out of which to construct with any definiteness the other life in which he believed. There is nothing very clear. As illustrating the general subject, let me leave Paul for a moment, and take up one or two passages written by other writers than Paul in different parts of the New Testament. The author of Second Peter—we do not know who he was—tells us that the world and everything connected with it is to be burned up. Some have supposed that this meant that it was to be consumed entirely ; others that it was to pass through a furnace of fire, be refined like gold, and come out cleansed and glorified,—a fit abode for the just. Others speak of the first heaven and the first earth as passing away, and new heavens and a new earth as being created. Others speak of the firmament as being rolled up like a scroll, and put away out of sight forever. And the author of the Book of Revelation gives us a beautiful, poetical picture of a fair city, pearl-gated, gold-streeted, filled with rivers of life and trees of life, descending out of heaven from God, and resting upon the earth.

We cannot with any certainty tell just what Paul's idea was. From all the hints we can gather, I am inclined to believe that Paul trusted that these resurrected souls should by and by be admitted into the presence-chamber of God in the heavens ; for he speaks in one place of his having been caught up in a vision into the third heaven, and of having seen wonderful things and heard wonderful words, which he was not permitted to repeat.

We are glad to find that Paul was a Universalist. It is very significant how strong his language is in this direction, and also how generally it has been overlooked by those who could find it in their hearts to believe the other horrible creed. Paul teaches that even the Jews—who were rejected on account of their rejection of Christ—were not to be finally passed by. They were rejected only for a time, until the fulness of the Gentiles was brought in. Then they also were to be gathered into one fold of God. Paul teaches with no questionable note that all souls—good and bad, Jew and Gentile, bond and free—are to be gathered at last into the one fold, with the one Shepherd.

And note that here, in connection with this Universalist tone, he records also his

Unitarian teaching. He says: Then comes the end, the climax of this great drama that has had the world for a stage, mountains for pillars, clouds for curtains, angels for spectators. Then comes the end, when Christ shall deliver up his kingdom to God the Father. He must reign until he has put everything under his feet—except God, the Power who put everything under him. When he has done that, when all rebellion, all power, all evil that opposes, is put down and is under the feet of the Christ, then he himself is to deliver up his kingdom to God, even the Father, and be subject to Him; and God is to be all and in all. This is the magnificent scheme of human history, and its outcome, that is taught us by the apostle Paul.

I wish now at the end to call your attention to two or three points that are instructive and full of meaning, and that throw light upon Paul's position. Paul teaches a doctrine, let me say in the first place, of utter unworldliness. He says we are not to be conformed to this world: we are to be transformed by the working of our minds, and lead a spiritual life. If we have money, we are to be as though we had none; if we are poor, we are not to be troubled by that; if we occupy a high position, it does not make any difference; if we occupy a low position, what matter? You remember that the slave-holders counted Paul as an ally, because he advised the escaped slave to return to his master: and I believe the old Abolitionists found it very hard to believe in Paul. But in the light of this consideration of Paul's doctrine we have found it divine, sweet, lovely in every way. What does it matter? Paul says. The second advent is nigh. It may be next week, next year, in two or three years, very soon, at any rate. What does it matter whether you are married or single, whether you are rich or poor, whether you are slave or master! These things are of no account. Bond and free, rich and poor, Jew and Gentile, all one in Christ, all brothers in him. These earthly conditions are of no account. It is not worth while to stop to try to change the social or political order. God will take care of that at the second advent, which is imminent at any moment. The more important thing for him to do was to proclaim this gospel over the world.

Note, in the second place, how superior Paul is to all suffering. He says, suppose you are sick, suppose you are persecuted, you are in pain, in tribulation: what matters it? Or he says, " Eye hath not seen, nor ear heard, neither hath entered into the heart of man, the things which God has prepared for those who love Him." Why worry about these things, then? " These light afflictions, which are but for a moment, work a far more exceeding and eternal weight of glory." Do you not see? If we believed that Christ was coming in a glory to flame from one end of heaven to the other, sounding the trump, raising the dead, leading us all into his eternal kingdom,—if that was a vivid belief of ours,—should we stop to whine or fret or trouble much over present conditions, whether we were sick or well, whether we were afflicted or free from affliction? Note the point of view of Paul. His attitude towards suffering and sickness and evil becomes grandly rational.

One other point. Here you see for the first time in the history of the world, granting his belief was reasonable, a magnificent triumph over death. And it was this victory over death more than anything else, than all things else combined, which gave young Christianity its victory over Rome. Why was it that, when these few feeble, unknown, despised disciples of an unknown peasant of Nazareth went forth into the mightiest empire of the world, they felt confident of taking possession? They visited city after city, preaching their news to the Jews who would listen, and then to the people of all nations; and they were persecuted. Persecuted, why? Not because Rome cared for any man's religion; but because a Christian could not consistently take part in the Roman public worship which Rome held to be the duty of every citizen. Rome persecuted the Christians, not primarily for their religion, but because they were bad Romans. These men could not worship with the Romans, because they had one Master in heaven, and Him only they worshipped; but they faced the mightiest power of earth, and they did it eagerly, with joy, with a song on their lips. What cared they, if they were sent to the wild beasts in the arena? They even coveted martyrdom. There are letters of certain old bishops, travelling through the empire on their way to Rome, who are anxious lest somehow or other they may escape martyrdom. They wanted to meet death. They wanted to be among the distinguished company in the other world of those who had died for the faith. Nothing that the Cæsar or any of his legions could do could strike even a momentary terror to their hearts; for they looked in the face of death, and they saw the coming of the heavenly legions, they heard the shout of the archangel, they listened for the trump that was to sound, they saw everywhere the dead rising from this underworld, they anticipated the transforming touch of the divine influence which was to clothe them with immortal life and beauty and glory ; and they looked forward to this as the one crown of a faithful life.

This, then, this heartening and giving hope to man, was that which conquered Rome ; for, as the centurions, the officers, the soldiers, the citizens, saw how men could live and love each other and serve each other, and how they did not care for riches or poverty, for high station or low, for pain, or for death, they said, What is the strange secret these men have found which delivers them from all that we have feared or cared for, and makes them victorious even in the face of the last dread enemy ? So at last Paul and his followers conquered the empire ; and, by this belief in the immortal life, they changed the face of civilisation and gave us the modern world.

V

JESUS AND IMMORTALITY

THE Second Epistle to Timothy, the first chapter, part of the tenth verse reads, " He hath abolished death, and hath brought life and immortality to light through the gospel."

We do not know who the writer of this Epistle may have been. Tradition ascribes it to Paul. At any rate, the writer holds substantially the Pauline view; and, when he says that Christ has abolished death and brought life and immortality to light, he speaks as one holding substantially the same ideas of the universe, of death and the future, as those which are set forth, in the preceding chapter, as belonging to Paul.

It seems strange at first sight that anyone should speak of Christ as having brought to light, or revealed, the immortal life, when, as we have seen, belief in this immortal life has been held from the very beginning of the world. Not a tribe, not a people, has been found who did not hold it in one form or another. In what sense, then, can the writer have meant to say that Christ brought it to light? The matter becomes clear when we remember that this writer, whoever he may have been, was unfamiliar with the historical facts which we have so briefly reviewed concerning the beliefs of other peoples; that he writes as a Hebrew, in the light of the Hebrew tradition. And, according to that tradition, all men from the beginning of time, at death, had gone down into this underworld of which I have spoken; and all of them had remained there until Christ, by the power conferred upon him as a gift from the Father, proved himself stronger than death, broke through its bonds, escaped, and led with him a multitude of those who up to that time had been held captive in this region below.

With that view of the universe, then, it appeared literally true that Christ was the one who first brought life and immortality to light.

In considering the opinions of Jesus we find a difficulty that did not present itself while we were dealing with the opinions of Paul. In treating these opinions we have Paul's own words to deal with. We have his letters, the clear and definite expression of his opinions.

But, when we come to deal with the Gospels, which were written, some of them, a good many years after the composition of the Pauline Epistles, we find ourselves front to front with this difficulty; it is easy enough to outline what the Gospels say concerning death and the future life; but we are not quite sure always that we are dealing with the precise and personal opinions of Jesus; for we have no letters of Jesus.　He wrote, so far as we know, not one single word,—left behind him no records except in the affectionate memories of those who had been his companions and followers.　See now how great this difficulty is.

It is about thirty-four years since Mr. Lincoln died.　He lived in an age of printing, of shorthand reporting.　He lived most conspicuous, lifted up in the eyes of mankind.　His most trivial sayings and doings were noted. It was supposed that they would become a part of history.　There are people living to-day who were intimately acquainted with him; and yet note this strange fact.　The other day, about the time when his birthday was celebrated, many sermons were preached in many different denominational pulpits in this city concerning the religious opinions of Mr. Lincoln.　When a Unitarian was preaching the sermon, Mr. Lincoln was a Unitarian. In Universalist pulpits he was a Universalist. In the orthodox churches he was good orthodox. In other words, thirty-four years after his death, people are already disputing as to his opinions, as to the religious theories he held, and as to what he said and did on a hundred different occasions.

Suppose now, for a moment, that there had been no printing-press at the time of Lincoln, that there had been no shorthand reporting, that he had never written a single letter or a single document of any kind,—do you not see how much greater would have been the probable confusion and contradiction as to what he really said, as to what he really did, as to what he really believed?

This is the position in which we are in regard to the sayings, the doings, the opinions of Jesus, only intensified by the fact that he lived two thousand years ago,—lived in the midst of an ignorant and very superstitious people, lived when there was no clear-cut distinction in the mind of any one between the natural and the supernatural, lived when anything might happen and when nothing was strange, or when, the stranger it appeared, the more likely it was to be accepted.

I speak of this so that you may note that there is possibly a very wide distinction between the teaching of the Gospels and the real opinions of Jesus. We know, for example, that Plato puts upon the lips of Socrates time after time his own opinions, or perhaps the opinions of Socrates modified and coloured, so that it is difficult to tell where Plato begins and Socrates leaves off. We know the same to be true in regard to the record concerning the life and the teachings of the Master. One great principle it will be well for you to bear in mind. If Jesus is reported as saying something which we know to have coincided with the popular opinion of his time, if he is reported as doing something that everybody expected the Messiah would do when he came, if he is reported as holding some opinion that the popular thought attributed to him as befitting the Messianic office, then you may be a little suspicious of this report.

That is, if there is any mistake anywhere, it would be likely to be in the direction of the popular expectation. But, when Jesus is reported as holding some opinion which was distinct, which was new, which cut across popular prejudices or went contrary to the expectation of his time, then you may feel practically certain that it is true that Jesus said or did that particular thing.

I needed to refer to this because sometimes in this chapter I shall be speaking of what I think Jesus really said, and sometimes I shall recur to the general testimony of the Gospels without drawing this particular line of de-markation ; but you need to have the idea in mind, if you wish to have clear thinking con-cerning what Jesus really held and really taught.

Now, I wish to note one other point. In view of the popular idea as to the nature and office of the Christ, one of the most remarkable things to me is his silences, his reticences. If he was what the popular theologians have said him to be, it seems very striking and strange in-deed that he did not say certain things about cer-tain matters concerning which he was perfectly silent. Let me instance two or three points.

It was the popular belief of his age that there had been a rebellion in heaven, and that the leader of this rebellion, with his followers, had been cast out into the abyss. Now, according to the popular conception of the office of Jesus, he was there. He was the first-born of all the angels. He was the bright archangel who led the divine power that put down and cast out these forces of evil. And yet he never anywhere makes the slightest allusion to it. He does not seem to have known anything about it. If he did, he did not consider it a matter of any importance, or, at any rate, did not consider it worth while that we should know about it. On this point he is utterly silent. Indeed, does it not seem to you a little significant and strange, if he had lived in heaven for uncounted ages before he appeared here, that he never says anything about what kind of place it was ? Even in the most intimate conversations with his disciples he does not allude to it. The silence seems to me very significant.

Another point concerning which he is equally reticent : he does not say a word about the Garden of Eden, the creation of Adam and Eve, the temptation, or the fall. And yet, according to the popular doctrine, he came here on purpose to deliver us from the results of these ; but he says nothing about them. I do not say that he did not believe this teaching : I simply say it is strange that he has nowhere made any mention of it.

Another point : Paul teaches, you know, with such force that he makes it the pivot on which his whole scheme of salvation turns, that death came into the world as the result of Adam's sin. Jesus says nothing whatever about the origin of death. He takes it for granted, of course; but he does not teach that it was the result of sin. He is utterly silent concerning the whole great, thrilling question. We may probably presume that he held this belief, because we know it was the popular belief of his time. Yet Jesus rose superior to the popular belief of his time in so many and in such marked directions that possibly we may find this to be only an illustration of that grand superiority which he so frequently manifested.

Now, let us turn and look the other way for a moment. What does Jesus teach as to the place of abode of the departed spirits? He teaches definitely nothing at all. He does make allusions to it, and these seem to show that he held the popular belief. For example, on the cross, when the penitent thief confesses his sins and prays for mercy, he says to him, "To-day shalt thou be with me in Paradise!" And Paradise, as we have seen, was one of the divisions of the underground world, the abode of departed spirits, the place where the good were permitted to go; while Gehenna was the place of abode of the bad.

I think I have already intimated to you that
the people held that these two places were
very close together,—Paradise and Gehenna ;
and this appears to be the thought of Jesus in
that famous parable of his concerning Dives
and Lazarus. There, you will remember,
Dives is in Gehenna, in the place of torment,
suffering, and longing for at least one drop of
water to cool his tongue ; and he looks and
sees Lazarus in Paradise, across the gulf fixed
between the two places.

In order to understand what it means for
the blessed to be in the bosom of Abraham,
you need to recall the attitude of those partaking of a feast in the olden time. They did
not sit in chairs around a table, but reclined
upon couches, or upon one long couch, lean-
ing on their left elbows near to the table, while
their feet extended away from the table towards the other part of the room. You will
see, in the light of this attitude, how easy it
was for the penitent Magdalen to come and
wash the feet of Jesus with her tears and wipe
them with the hairs of her head while he was
reclining, not sitting, at the table. The intimate friend of someone thus at the board
would be next to him, just in front of him, able
to turn and look into his face, and, as it were,

lean upon his bosom. And this, of course, was the sign of the greatest favour that could be conferred upon one,—to be thus intimately related to a great or distinguished person on a festival occasion like this. Heaven—or the abode of the blessed—is frequently described under this figure of a feast, and those that are saved are spoken of as reclining in the bosom of Abraham. So Jesus represented Lazarus, the beggar, as at last lifted to this sublime felicity, and Dives, the rich man, so near to him that he can see him—so near that they can converse back and forth over the gulf of separation. This throws light upon the conception which Jesus held of the under-world, and shows that he shared the opinions of his time, or, at least, was willing to use those opinions for illustrating his truth when he gave utterance to this remarkable parable.

The only other phase that I need to note is one which will lead us, significantly, to a higher teaching on the part of Jesus than we have noted in regard to his disciples. Notice his conversation with those who were about him just before the crucifixion, as it is recorded in the Gospel according to John. He says that he is going away, he is going to the Father; that he goes to prepare a place for them; and that, when he has prepared a place for them, he will come again and receive them to himself, that they may always be together. You see, he touches here a point which is often mooted in the theological discussions of the world, as to our recognising friends who have preceded us into this other life. If we are to accept the teaching of Jesus as of authority, then those who have been intimately associated here will naturally gravitate together in that spiritual life and will renew the felicity and the sweetness of their old-time associations. He is coming to take his friends to the place he has prepared for them ; and they are ever to be together in the sweetness of a love untouched by pain, unshadowed by the possibility of another separation through death.

But now there is a very striking thing to be noted. In the midst of this conversation he says, " Whither I go ye know, and the way ye know." But Thomas said, " We know not whither thou goest, and how can we know the way ? " Then what does he answer ? He does not say that it is in the underworld ; he does not say it is above the sky ; he does not say it is off on some distant star in space ; he does not point in any direction, east, west, north, or south. He simply says, " I am the way."

Spiritually interpreted, meaning simply this spiritual, divine truth which he embodied, which he represented, and which he had been teaching,—this is the way to the eternal felicity, this is the way to the home of the blessed.

You see he is touching on mystical ground, he is coming to the utterance of a most profound and significant spiritual truth. For, in another place, when he is speaking of eternal life, he does not say it is the living in a walled city, or in a beautiful palace, or in the midst of fadeless trees and luscious fruits. He says, "This is eternal life, to know Thee, the only true God, and Jesus Christ whom Thou has sent." In other words, eternal life is a quality, in the teaching of Jesus. It is a matter of character, it is spiritual unfolding, it is insight, it is being,—not simply place nor surrounding.

I must touch on one subject for a moment, though giving no decisive opinion on it, because I hold none. The parable of Dives and Lazarus suggests inevitably the question as to whether Jesus believed not only in the immortal life, but in the immortal death,—whether he believed in eternal punishment, in other words. You know very well what a conflict of opinion there has been in regard to this matter.   Jesus uses words which can very easily be interpreted in favour of endless punishment, or, at least, words that can be so interpreted are attributed to him.   But we must remember two or three things.

In the first place, we are never quite certain as to whether these opinions may not have been coloured by the belief of the age when the Gospels took their present shape.   Then we must remember that Jesus was an Oriental : he spoke in figure, he used poetical expressions ; and the tendency of the Protestant theologian is to harden these flowers and figures of speech down into cold, hard, literal prose. Let me suggest to you this matter by recurring to the words of Mozoomdar, the famous East Indian seer, when he was in this country two years ago.   " Jesus," he said, " was an Oriental ; and we Orientals understand him.   He spoke in figure. We understand him. He was a mystic.   You take him literally : you make an Englishman of him."   This was his judgment as to the way in which we are apt to interpret the sayings of Jesus. We must remember that, then.   And how much of this is simply striking poetical figure of speech, and how much is literal verity, it is very difficult for us at present to say.

And then we must remember that Jesus, a great many times, was talking of the end of the age, the great transition that was believed to be imminent at the time of the coming of the Messiah, and not of the final condition of things when the heavens and the earth should have passed away.

It seemed to me necessary to recur to this point for a moment; but I am inclined to believe that Jesus held such a doctrine of the infinite love of the Father as would preclude the possibility of holding to that which seems to us the inevitable and eternal contradiction of that love. And let me say again, as a matter of perfect honesty, that, if the doctrine of eternal punishment was clearly and unmistakably taught on every leaf of the Bible and on every leaf of all the Bibles of all the world, I could not believe a word of it. I should appeal from these misconceptions of even the seers and the great men to the infinite and eternal Good, who only is God, and who only on such terms could be worshipped.

I must refer now to that which is in some ways the very central teaching of Jesus; and you will see that, though it appears to be going away from our theme for a moment, it is coming back to the very heart of it. The one thing that Jesus preached and taught first and foremost, in the presence of which everything else was subsidiary, was his doctrine of the kingdom of God. His first word is, "The kingdom of heaven is at hand." And this doctrine of the kingdom he preaches first, last, and all the time. It was to set up this kingdom that, he tells us, he came.

It is very curious to note what a strange transformation the teaching of Jesus has undergone at the hands of those who have claimed to be his interpreters. The kingdom of God in the modern world, the perfect kingdom of God, is the few people who belong to the particular church of the one who happens to be writing about it, or those churches which are in general sympathy with it ; while the final, complete salvation which Jesus had in mind when he spoke of the kingdom of God and its citizens, has been postponed to another world. We look for a perfect condition of things only after death. Jesus looked for it here. There is no slightest reason whatever for supposing that Jesus expected the perfect kingdom of heaven, of which he talked, to be established anywhere else except on this poor old earth of ours. That judgment scene of his, where he represents the conditions of entering into that kingdom, is worthy of our notice. What does he say about the conditions?

Now, I am not going to say a word against church or Bible, ritual or service. But I wish you to see carefully this : when Jesus is discussing the terms of admission to his perfect kingdom, he does not say a word about belonging to a church, does not refer to it. He does not say a word about your belief, as to whether or no you have any creed, or as to whether, if you have, it is correct. No reference to it. He does not say anything about a sacrament. He does not refer to the Bible, to reading it or neglecting it ; not a hint as to prayer,—absolutely not one word concerning any of those things which are ordinarily set off by themselves and classed as religious duties. The only condition of admittance to his kingdom of heaven, which he has come to set up, is simple human goodness,—not the slightest hint of anything else.

And where is this kingdom to be established? Right here. He says, " The kingdom of heaven cometh not by observation. If they say, Lo, here, or Lo, there, pay no attention to them ; for the kingdom of God, is within you," or, as it may equally well be translated, —and note that it does not essentially change its meaning,—" is among you." That is, the kingdom of God is right here already, it is begun, it is in any true and noble heart.

This chimes in with the doctrine of his conversation with the woman of Samaria. He says, It is not in this mountain, Gerizim, where you worship, it is not in Jerusalem, it is not in any particular place in the world where shrines are set up and special rites celebrated, that you can find God. " God is Spirit ; and they that worship Him must worship Him in spirit and in truth." And His kingdom is wherever a single heart loves and worships in spirit and in truth. It is right here in this world.

And now note one more point. When is the change coming that is to set up this kingdom? For, contradictory as it may seem, if the reports of Jesus are accurately made, he teaches that this kingdom is not a matter of slow growth, spreading from one heart to another as goodness naturally grows, by contagion, but it is to be set up by divine intervention at his own second coming, at a time when all nature is to be convulsed, the stars are to fall from heaven, everything is to be shaken. Then the trumpet is to sound ; and he, accompanied by his legions of angels, is to appear in the sky, and the old is to pass away and the new is to be established. He says definitely that " This generation shall not pass away until all these things be fulfilled."

I have very serious doubt myself as to whether Jesus did say this. We know this to have been the popular belief of his time; and, very likely, this popular belief gets into the reported saying, when he himself did not use the precise language that is here imputed to him. But, at any rate, we know that he did teach the immediate coming of this kingdom, that it was to be established here on earth, and that the simple, human, lovable, good were to be its citizens.

Now, at the end, I have two or three points which I wish to make, which I believe to be only fair and just and true, as pointing to the very heart and significance of the teaching of Jesus. I have already touched on the matter; but I wish to emphasise it by setting it apart as a point by itself. Jesus teaches that the eternal life is a matter of quality, of character, and that there are people all around us now living the eternal life; that it is not a question simply of duration. If we are to take these words of Jesus with the full power of their meaning, a man might keep on living forever and never know anything about the eternal life; as, for example, you can conceive of an animal, a horse, or a dog, as living on indefinitely, but as knowing nothing of any high human life.

This eternal life is of higher grade, of finer quality than the ordinary life of men and women. And what is the essence of it? It is that the person comes to live in those things which are eternal, which are deathless in their very nature, which are divine, partaking of the divine quality. Paul says that knowledge, for example, can pass away. In other words, if I live, I may be perfect in my knowledge of the geography of this planet; but, suppose I move to another planet, that is of no more value to me. So a large part of the knowledge over which we labour may be of a great deal of importance to us to-day, and yet not permanent in its nature. But Paul says that faith and hope and love abide. These are the things that last. All those divine qualities and characteristics that make us like God,—these are the things that are imperishable, that endure forever and ever. And the man that comes up to the high level of this kind of life, and tastes these things, is tasting to-day the eternal life.

Thus it is in accord, I think, with the deepest teaching of Jesus that we should remember how shallow and false our conception of a future life is. There is no such thing as a " future " life in the sense in which we talk about it. There is no past except in our memory. There is no to-morrow except in our anticipation. The whole universe lives this instant, and only this instant. We are in the immortal life now. If we are naturally immortal, death will make no change in us : it is a mere incident in our career.

So Jesus teaches, I think, that the eternal life, being a quality of character, exists to-day. It is not something to be waited for. Our friends, for example, if they are alive anywhere, are alive at all, are alive this minute. They are not alive in the future somewhere any more than a friend who has gone to Europe is living in a future life.

Do not let us be deluded by the superficial meaning of words. We are the children of God. We are immortal this moment ; and, though here on this planet, and encased in these bodies, we are living the immortal life. Let us rise to the level, then, of what Jesus means by the eternal life, and be worthy of it.

And there is another thing, which we seem to suppose (those of us who believe in it at all) to have been peculiar to the dispensation of two thousand years ago. This every-day, common-place world of hopes and fears, meetings and partings, joys and sorrows,—this world, according to the Gospel story, is encased in a world of spirit, immersed in it, surrounded by it as by an atmosphere. I am not now saying that I believe this, I am not saying that you believe it. I say it is the Gospel conception.

Note, before Jesus comes into this world at all, messengers from the Unseen appear, and report that he is coming. He is guarded in his childhood, he is watched over all the way along. When he appears at the Jordan for baptism, out of the closely enfolding invisible comes the appearance of a dove, figuring forth the Spirit ; and a voice is heard saying, " This is my beloved Son." He gets weary : messengers out of the Unseen appear and minister to him. And so all the way along,—appearances, visions, voices. His disciples go one day with him up on a mountain-top, and suddenly they see him surrounded by a glory that they have never seen before ; and, as they gaze, two forms that they recognise afterwards as being Moses and Elijah, appear and talk with him. They disappear again, the vision vanishes. After his resurrection some of his disciples are walking along a road towards Emmaus; and he suddenly appears, and talks to them. Then he reveals himself to them in breaking of bread, and disappears again. On another occasion he appears suddenly to his disciples while they are behind closed doors in an upper room, and then fades away out of their sight. And after he has finally disappeared into the invisible, two shining ones appear to the disciples as they watch his departure, and tell them that it will not be a great while before they see his return out of the invisible again.

The point I wish you to notice is, that, according to the conception of the Gospels, the fundamental Christian conception of the other world is that it is close by, all around us; and the life of Jesus is full of visions, of voices, appearances, manifestations, warnings, helpings, guidings, from this other life, in which, as I said, the universe seems to be immersed.

So the real life, according to the teaching of Jesus, is this spirit life, this life for which we are now in training, this life which deals with the high and fine, and sweet and pure, this life that is one of love, of service, of self-forgetfulness, of consecration to others; and the things that people care the most about, are apt to care the most for, are perishable, and pass away with the using. The eternal life, according to Jesus, is the only true human life, the one to which we ought to consecrate ourselves here and now.

VI

THE OTHER WORLD OF THE MIDDLE AGES

IF we could wake up for a little while in the Middle Ages,—say the tenth, eleventh, twelfth or thirteenth century,—I fear we should not find it a pleasant time in which to be alive. The world was a scene of political disorder, contention on every hand. But, worse than that, it was brooded over by supernatural fears,—fears wide and dark-winged, that shadowed the lives and shut out the sunshine from the souls of men. God was away off in the empyrean, never seen, rarely felt to be nigh to men. He was to be approached only through a series of mediators. First, indeed, the Church had taught that His Son, the second person in the Trinity, had come to reveal Him. But it was hundreds of years since the Son was here; and he had withdrawn into the heavens, and was now seated at the right hand of God. And, when next he came, it was not to be chiefly on an errand of mercy, but as the severe Judge of all the earth.

Human hearts, feeling the need of something tender and human in the divinity, had transformed Mary from being merely a peasant woman of Nazareth into the Mother of God. And they felt that they could appeal to her tenderness and love; and they could hope that she would intercede with the Son, who would intercede with the Father, who might come to care for them.

And then, as Mary sometimes was far away, as she grew and was exalted into a dignity that was attached to her as the Mother of God, they drew nigh to certain saints,— men who had been distinguished for charity and kindliness and love when on earth, and who had been set apart as specially holy and helpful since they had entered into the Unseen. And so, as I say, God was a long way off, only to be approached through saints, through the Virgin, through Jesus.

But, while God was at a distance, the devils were very, very near. The air about the earth was supposed to be full of these evil, tempting spirits. They caused shipwreck at sea and sudden death on land; they blighted the crops; they smote and blasted in the tempests;

they took possession of the bodies and the souls of men. They were ever ready—as in the case of Faust—to enter into a compact with a man, bestowing upon him whatever earthly blessing he might desire, and, in lieu of that, taking a mortgage on his soul.

The devils, then, were very near ; and God was very far.

The two worlds interpenetrated each other, but more frequently, perhaps, for evil than for good. Not always for evil, for sometimes the Virgin Mary was seen, at least in a vision, sometimes the angels manifested themselves for human help ; but the two worlds, as I said, interpenetrated each other. And this, note, all the way along from the very beginning of human history. In every religion there has been possible communion between the seen and the unseen.

In order now that we may comprehend the kind of world that the people lived in, during the Middle Ages, and that you may see how natural it was that the ideas I have already spoken of were popularly held, I need to picture to you in outline the universe as it was believed to be during these centuries. And I take for my purpose the world of Dante. I do this merely because Dante has given it to us in clear-cut outline more plainly than we find it in most other writings. I do it because, not only has Dante given us the figure of the external universe as it was believed in by the scholars of his time, but he has summed up the philosophy, the theology, all the wisdom of the Middle Ages,—in this, his marvellous poem,—as you can find them nowhere else. I take him, then, as a type, and for the purposes of illustration.

The theory of the universe held at that time, and thus outlined by Dante, was, as you well know, what has been called the Ptolemaic theory, that one which has been displaced during the last four hundred years by the Copernican. That you may locate the time a little more definitely, I will remind you of the fact that Dante was born sometime during the year 1265, and that he died in the early part of the fourteenth century.

The earth was a sphere, a globe,—at the centre of the universe. It was the centre of gravity of the universe,—the one spot, and the only spot, that was at rest. There was land on one of its hemispheres and water on the other. Now, around this earth were the different crystal concentric spheres. We talk now of the spheres, of the music of the spheres;

but the old meaning has been completely discharged from those phrases, and it is hard for us, even imaginatively, to appreciate what was the belief of that time.

You are to think of nine or ten concentric crystallised spheres, as real as a nest of glass globes, each inside the other. There was first the sphere of the Moon, as the body nearest to the earth. Then the sphere of Mercury, then of Venus. Then the Sun, regarded at that time as a planet. Then Mars, Jupiter, Saturn. These were the seven planets known ; and each of these was supposed to be attached to one of these crystal globes or spheres, and these turned around the earth, and carried the planets with them in their motions. It was in this way that the Ptolemaic astronomers explained the movements of the heavenly bodies.

Outside of these came next another sphere, in which were all the fixed stars in one plane. Beyond that was what was called the Primum mobile, the first one of the spheres that moved. And beyond that was the Empyrean, unmoved, beyond space, beyond time, in eternity.

Above the Empyrean were nine other circles, or spheres, representing the angelic hierarchy. There were nine orders of angels. These were the Seraphim, the Cherubim, the

Throne,—three. Then were the Dominations, the Virtues, the Powers,—three others. Then the Principalities, Archangels, Angels. Three times three great circuits or rings, in which abode the angels, according to their rank and order.

The Seraphim, in the smaller circle, were nearest the centre of life and power in the universe where God was at the same time manifested and hidden in His ineffable glory. Then these spheres radiated farther and farther from God, and came nearer and nearer to the world. Dante tells us that the angels and the spheres that made up the universe as it was believed in at his day were created at the same time. And the reason for it is this: the angels in their rank moved—receiving their power from God, and their motion and life from Him, in their order — and controlled the different spheres that made up the world. That is, the Seraphim moved the highest sphere, the outermost one, that of Saturn; the Cherubim moved the next one within, that of Jupiter; and so on in their order clear down. And Dante tells us that they must have been created at the same time; because, if the worlds had been made without the angels, there would have been nothing to move the worlds;

and, if the angels had been created without the spheres of the worlds, there would have been nothing for them to do; so their creation was coincident in time.

Here, then, is an outline of the kind of universe that people supposed they lived in during the Middle Ages. But now we come to a tremendous change.

As you see, there were just these spheres of the different planets, and these rings or circles in which dwelt the angels, with God at the centre. But what is the result when the angels are created, according to Dante? It was just twenty seconds, as Dante tells us, after the angels were created, that Lucifer rebelled, leading a third part of the angels with him; and they were cast out into the abyss. Only twenty seconds; and his cause of the rebellion was different from that which Milton gives us at a later time. It was not ambition: according to Dante, it was impatience to know everything all at once, and because God did not confer upon Lucifer perfect knowledge soon enough, he rebelled against God's authority and was cast out.

Now there came a great change in the earth, caused by the fall of the angels. When Satan, the great leader, fell, he struck the earth at a

point which later became the precise place
where the temple in Jerusalem was located.
The earth, in horror and fear, fled at his approach ; and so, as he fell, it shrunk away from
him, and created a tunnel reaching from the
surface of the earth down to precisely the centre, the centre of gravity.   And here, because
it was the centre of gravity, Satan stuck fast,
and has been imprisoned there in eternal ice
from that day to this.   Satan, then, was poised
just at the centre of gravity of the world ; and
so much of the earth as had filled up this tunnel and had fled at his approach, sunk through
the planet, and emerged as an enormous mountain on the other side, the only land in all the
western hemisphere.   And at the summit of
this mountain, which became the Mount of
Purgatory, was located the earthly Paradise.

When Adam and Eve were created, they
were placed here in the Garden of Eden, on
the summit of this mountain.   But how long
was it before they fell?   A little longer than
the angels.   The angels, as I told you, kept
their first estate only twenty seconds.   Adam
and Eve maintained their innocence seven
hours ; that was all.   When I read the story
in the Old Testament, and see that Adam was
put to sleep and Eve created, and that he

named all the animals and did a good many other remarkable things, it impresses me that that must have been a busy seven hours for him. But in seven hours he was cast out of the Garden of Eden.

Dante does not explain it; but it becomes a problem as to how, since the Garden of Eden was located on the top of a lofty mountain, in the midst of a hemisphere of water on the opposite side of the globe, the human race is found to have its original home on the eastern hemisphere, in Asia. So one tradition has it that the human race lived there on what came to be the Purgatorial Mountain, until after the flood, and that, when the ark took Noah and his family away from this mountain, it floated around the world, and at last landed them on Mount Ararat, in Asia; and so the original location of Paradise became lost to the world.

This is the kind of world, then, that we find was believed in during the Middle Ages.

Now, I wish to take you on a little tour with me. I shall make it as short as I may, and have it comprehensible to you.

Dante goes to hell, climbs the Mount of Purgatory, and is admitted even into the angelic spheres and among the blessed who are enjoying the Beatific Vision. In other words, he makes a pilgrimage throughout the known universe of his time. And after his great poem was written it is said that the women and the children would point fearsome fingers at him as they saw him with his eternally sad face and bowed head going through the streets, and say, "There is a man whose beard was singed on his journey through hell," so real did this journey seem to the imaginations of the people of the time.

This poem of Dante's is one of the half-dozen greatest poems of all the world. In it he sums up the philosophy, the theology, the science,—all the wisdom of his time. It is so interfused with Dante's magnificent qualities of soul, it is so touched by his feelings of pity for human sorrow, it is so dreadful in its pictorial representation of the results of human sin, that it can never be forgotten or cease to be one of the treasures of the world.

Let us accompany Dante briefly in his journey through hell and up the Mount of Purgatory. He finds himself, he says, lost in a thick wood. Three wild beasts meet him,—the allegorical significance of these we need not trouble ourselves about now,—and he is about to turn back in fear when he sees Virgil,— Virgil who, in the popular imagination of the people in the Middle Ages, was made a magus, and a wonder-worker of every kind, whom Dante regards as perhaps the greatest poet of all antiquity, and had recognised as his master. Virgil tells him that Beatrice, the one whom he loved so passionately in his youth, who had died, and whom now he worshipped as an emblem and symbol of divine philosophy, had sent him to take him on this journey through the other world, that he might learn its lessons and teach them to his people.

So, as they go on, they come at last to that gate which the world will never forget, over which is the inscription, " All hope abandon, ye who enter here." Dante declares—and he tried to believe it—that it was written that both Love and Wisdom were engaged in building this prison ; but the part of the inscription which no one ever overlooks is that which I have quoted.

They find themselves in the first circle of hell, a sort of ante-hell,—an outermost circle, an entrance-way, a porch,—not hell as a place of torment yet. And here whom do they find, before they have really entered the place of excruciating anguish ? Dante finds that this is the abode of Virgil himself, his loved and revered master. And he finds here Socrates, finds here all the great, the noble, the good, the famous, of the ancient world,—not one of them with any chance of salvation. And yet Dante could not quite put them into a place of positive torment. They suffer simply with a deathless though hopeless longing,—longing for God, longing for light, longing for peace. And these are never to be attained. For Dante teaches us that, no matter how good, no matter how true, no matter how noble a man may have been, there is no possibility of salvation for him unless he foresaw Christ, and believed in him, or else looked back to Christ, and believed in him, and was baptised.

Here also is an innumerable company of innocent, prattling babes that can never enter heaven. Why?

We are taught that before circumcision was heard of, if a parent had wonderful faith in God and did the best he could, his child might be saved. After circumcision was revealed to the Jews, no babe in all the world could possibly be saved unless it had been circumcised. And, after baptism had been given, no babe in all the world had any hope unless it had been baptised. So here, in the ante-hell, were all the good of the antique world and the millions on millions of babes with no hope for any of them in the theology of that time.

Then the fearful descent begins. I need not tell you—you know—how, in circle after circle, as they went down lower and lower, the quality of the sin is supposed to be increased, and the excess of the torment to be intensified. Tortures horrible, unspeakable, almost unreadable, fill the description of the mediæval hell, until we come, as I said, to the bottom. There is Satan, so large, Dante says, that one of his arms was as much larger than a giant as a giant was larger than he. He has three faces ; and Judas Iscariot is being mangled in one of his mouths, and Brutus and Cassius each in one of the others. This peculiar punishment for Brutus and Cassius grows out of Dante's political philosophy. He had what he thought was a sufficient reason for placing them there.

Then begins a new experience to this pilgrim in the other world. He starts, as he supposes, to climb down the thighs of Satan, but suddenly finds himself climbing up. He does not understand what it means until Virgil explains that he has passed the centre of gravity, and is ascending towards the other surface of the world.

They find four rivers in hell, caused by the

tears of anguish and suffering and sorrow and shame that have afflicted the world. They follow up the channel, worn by another river; and this one flows, they find, from purgatory, and is caused by the tears of penitence of those that are ascending its mount. They come to the shores of the island from which this mountain rises, and there begin the ascent. Here there are seven circles, corresponding to the seven cardinal sins as taught by the Catholic Church. When they reach the Garden of Eden, or the Earthly Paradise on the summit, Virgil suddenly disappears. He can go no farther; and Beatrice, who has come down from her angelic circle, meets him, and becomes his guide through the celestial spheres.

In these spheres of the angels, the position which the saved souls occupy corresponds again to Dante's idea of divine justice. Those who had been most worthy, who deserved most, who were most distinguished for piety, are placed in the highest circles, and nearest to God. At the very centre—the light reflected in a wondrous lake—is the glory that hides the Triune God. Sometimes the blessed that are close to Him are permitted a glimpse of that ineffable radiance which would blind those who are not prepared for the vision.

Here then is Dante's universe. It is on a pilgrimage like this that he travelled through hell, up the Mount of Purgatory, and into the heavens.

Now, I wish to note certain characteristics of it which seem to me important that we should touch upon, and the lessons which we should learn therefrom. When Dante sees these souls in hell, they are embodied, after a fashion. They looked to him just as they did when he used to meet them on the streets of Florence. And yet they do not need to eat or drink : their bodies are not like the fleshly bodies that they had in this world ; but at the same time they are capable of suffering unspeakable anguish,—hunger, thirst, cold, heat, stinging winds. Only, remember, this hell is not quite complete, and heaven is not quite complete, until after the resurrection of the body and the final judgment, because a man is not supposed to be able to suffer everything of which he is capable until he is a whole man, body and soul together ; and he is not supposed to be capable of enjoying all that is best until he is a whole man after the same fashion.

I want you to note here something that seems to me pathetic. I have studied all the old religions of the world ; but Christianity is distinguished from all others—and it is a lamentable distinction,—as being the *first* religion on the face of the earth that ever taught immortal, hopeless anguish. The other religions have their hells,—infinitely horrible, tortures such as we cannot conceive ; but they always think of time as made up of cycles, and those cycles come to an end. So all the hells end sometime, with the exception of the Christian hell. There is no other hell that I know of that does not come to an end.

And this hell, as I said a moment ago, includes all the noblest of the heathen as well as the worst of them, and includes all the unbaptised children that have ever been born and have died.

There is a characteristic now of purgatory that I wish to speak of ; and, to lead to it, let me say this : I presume my experience in trying to read Dante is very much like that of the experience of the average man. I have loved poetry from the time I was able to read at all. I read all the old English poets,— finding them in our own little town library,— read them over and over before I had the slightest idea as to their relative rank and importance. I say this merely to show that what I have to say now does not spring out of the fact that I have no love for poetry. I have always loved it almost more than anything else in literature.

When I began to read Dante, I found his *Hell* interesting. It was terribly interesting; but it was real, it was human. You had seen the people, you had heard them talk. I read *Purgatory* with a good deal less interest and with much more difficulty. It did not seem half so human to me : there was an air of artificiality about it. And I believe in purgatory, not as a place, but as a condition of experience both in this world and the next. But I believe that people are to work out their salvation, deliverance from their wickedness and their sins, through genuine practice of goodness in the helping of others, not in gymnastic exercises that have no unselfish purpose; no purpose beyond themselves. Now, purgatory is simply a moral gymnasium in Dante. Those who are punished go through many tortures; but that does not help anybody else, does not make the world any better, does not do any good except to provide so much torture for so many sins while in the world below; so that purgatory always seemed to me unreal, unnatural.

There is another defect about it. The Catholic Church, I have no doubt, meant well ; but, for example, if a man was saved at last,—that is, if he got a chance to go to purgatory, which always meant a chance to get out of it and go to paradise and be among the saved,—if he postponed his repentance until the last day of his life, he would be delayed in the ante-purgatory which preceded the purgatory proper for thirty years for every single year of his postponement in the matter of repentance. But the prayers of his friends and those who loved him could expedite that journey and shorten the time. So here you find all the prayers and the masses of the Catholic Church from the beginning for the deliverance of men from purgatory ; and it has been perhaps, the grandest of all the Catholic Church's sources of revenue. This is a serious criticism on the purgatory of the Church.

As I said, I read the *Inferno* with intense interest. I read the *Purgatorio* with less interest ; and the *Paradiso* was the most uninteresting of the three. None of the heavens that orthodox Christendom has offered to us has ever been interesting to me. In Dante's universe the only reason I can imagine for anyone's ever wanting to get to heaven is for the sake of getting out of the other place. There is nothing for him to do: there is nothing human for him to be engaged in.

Now, let us review some of the other religions, and see how much more natural they are in this respect. Go back to the traditional spirit world of the Indians. When the Indian got to his happy hunting grounds, he was happy. He had his dogs and horses, his bows and arrows, and was able to do something that he liked to do. Then take the Walhalla of the Norseman,—not, perhaps, a very elevating life, that of being engaged in mortal combat with one another; but it was something to appeal to and thrill the rough bravery of the Norsemen. So take any of the other religions of the world with which I am acquainted, and there is something to go to heaven for, something to do after you get there; but the old heaven that I used to hear pictured as a boy, the heaven described as a place where man was to play on harps and listen to celestial music forever, was not an attractive place. I remember when I used to hear the hymn sung, one verse of which closed with

" Where congregations ne'er break up,
And sabbaths never end."

I used to think I would almost rather go anywhere else than there.

And so, when we come to Dante's heaven, the spirits discuss scholastic philosophy, fine points of theology; and they gain now and then glimpses of what Dante tells us causes inexpressible bliss : the Beatific Vision. But it means nothing to us. I cannot understand what is meant by the Beatific Vision, or why it should cause exquisite delight ; therefore, Dante's heaven has no meaning, and so no attraction. To have any attraction for me, heaven must be a place of growth, of progress. One must be able there to find scope and room for the exercise of every grand and fine faculty of human nature.

One question Dante asks there, and he receives no answer. I have told you that Dante seemed to be troubled because the great and noble of the ancient world must stay forever in hell ; but it was church doctrine, and Dante was orthodox. He did not dare to contradict the teachings of his Church. He asks one of the old philosophers and wise men of the Church why it is ? The only answer he gets is the one that Paul offers to the man who asks questions : " Who art thou that repliest against God ? " He gets no explanation ; and

Dante shows that he comes away with an aching heart, because he, the Florentine, was infinitely better than his God.

This doctrine of everlasting punishment is blasphemy against God, is an outrage on every sentiment of justice, is a ghastly denial of the divine love ; and it has been the cause of more wars, of more hatred, of more bloodshed, on this poor old earth of ours, than any other one thing conceivable. It has been because men have said, " If these people hold and cherish such ideas, they will go to hell, and they will take thousands and millions of other people to hell with them ; we must stop it at any cost." This has been the reason why thinking and daring have been accounted crime. The Bloody Mary of England reasoned logically when she said, " It is fit that I should burn these heretics here, whom my God is to burn in the other world forever and ever." Why should she be any better than her God ? And, if it were true, then the suppression of heresy at any cost was mercy. There has never been a rack nor a thumb-screw, there has never been an *auto-da-fé*, there has never been any one of the horrors of the Inquisition, there has never been murder like that of the Waldenses, never a fire at Smithfield, never a persecution from the date of the birth of the gentle Jesus until now,—now, when we are getting back the gentle Jesus again,—that has not been caused by this infernal doctrine of divine hate.

Let us, then, be thankful for the changes of human thought that have given us a better heaven than that of Dante, and that have blotted out forever the hideousness of his hell.

VII

PROTESTANT BELIEF CONCERNING DEATH AND THE LIFE BEYOND

THE first verse from the twenty-first chapter of the Book of Revelation reads : " And I saw a new heaven and a new earth : for the first heaven and the first earth were passed away ; and there was no more sea."

We do not know who may have been the author of this Book of Revelation. Traditionally, it has been assigned to John, the favourite, among the apostles. The best scholarship of the age, however, is inclined to think that originally it was a Jewish treatise, antedating the birth of Christ, and that afterwards it was worked over by some Christian hand and brought into its present shape. This is the belief of the best scholarship of the age. I have made no such careful study of it myself as to be able—even if it were required—to tell you what parts of it are Jewish and what parts Christian. I wish simply to say that the writer, whoever he may have been, marks in his statements a transition time between the old thought of the heavens and the earth and the new. He declares the first heaven and the first earth to have passed away, and says that he sees—doubtless in vision, looking down the future—new heavens and a new earth. In this new heaven and new earth there is to be no more sea.

Let me say, in passing, that friendship and love for the sea are comparatively modern. In nearly all the classic literature of the world you find it referred to as a barren and desolate waste. It was also looked on as a barrier between peoples, so standing in the way of human inter-knowledge and human brotherhood.

The seer saw a time when the old heaven and the old earth would pass away and all things would become new. We are to consider a part at least of this transition epoch, and note to what a remarkable extent and in what ways the old heavens and the old earth are gone, and new heavens and a new earth have taken their places.

Partly by way of comparison and partly for the sake of making this transition statement gentle and easy, it seems to me worth while to consider for a little the universe of Milton, the other great epic poet who has made us so much at home in imaginative other worlds.

Dante's theory of the universe was that of Ptolemy. I tell you substantially the same concerning Milton's; and yet Milton modifies in some very important particulars the thought of Dante. Milton stands in a peculiar relation to the universe of Ptolemy and the new theory of Copernicus. Copernicus was born before Milton, and published his book long before Milton's birth. Milton was perfectly familiar with the new speculation of Copernicus. He had probably seen Galileo in Italy, the man who had done so much to establish the Copernican theory in the popular imagination. And yet at that time, the time of Milton, the whole Copernican universe was looked upon by the people very much as Darwinism is looked upon to-day. Scholars, those who understood Copernicus and were able to comprehend his reasonings and his proofs, had no doubt of its truth.

So those to-day who have studied and who comprehend Darwin, and are able to estimate his reasonings and his proofs, have no question about the essential truth of Darwinism. But there are people to-day by the thousand who have not done Mr. Darwin the honour to comprehend him, and so do not accept his teaching. So there were thousands in the time of Milton who, not having done Copernicus the honour to comprehend him, did not accept his teaching. They still clung to the old Ptolemaic theory of the universe; and Milton clings to it, at least so far as his poetical purpose is concerned. We are not sure, we have no way of knowing, whether Milton really accepted the theory of Copernicus or not. He does not tell us; but he recognises it as a speculation in his verse. He makes Adam talk with one of the angels concerning this new theory. But it is very curious. The same old note that rings from the beginning all up the ages is struck: the angel advises Adam not to pry too curiously into these matters; to be modest and accept the teachings of the Church and look after the welfare of his soul, and leave these things to the constituted authorities. This is the advice that has been given to man from the beginning; and, thank God, it is the advice that man has never taken.

Milton, then, accepted the Ptolemaic theory as the frame-work of his great epic; and, in order that it may be compared with that of

Dante, let me outline a few of its main features.

Of course, there was no purgatory in Milton's universe, because purgatory was a Catholic doctrine which the Protestants rejected. There was only place for earth and heaven and hell. Imagine me drawing here, a large circle ; within that circle would be contained the entire Miltonic universe. Let me now draw a line across the centre, like an equator on a map of the hemisphere ; and all above that equatorial line would be the empyrean, or heaven, the abode of God and the angels, and afterwards of the saved. Below that was chaos. After the war in heaven, when the angels were cast out, they fell through this chaos ; and, to give you an idea of the size of Milton's universe, it took them just nine days and nights to fall from the empyrean to the bottom. They fell to the bottom of this circle ; after that, a dome was suddenly created, formed like the antarctic circle on a hemispherical map. Beneath this antarctic circle was hell. The remainder of the space beneath the empyrean was chaos.

God then determined to create the world and man. And remember that, in those days, the word "world" was not identical with the word "earth." The world included all the physical universe, the planets and stars. God, then, created the world. And, in order to represent the size of the world, imagine a small circle, the top of which would just touch the floor of the empyrean, and the bottom of which would reach half-way down to the antarctic circle, the top, or roof, of hell. Within this ring there were the nine concentric crystalline spheres that you remember were described in Dante's universe,—the spheres of the Moon, Mercury, Venus, Sun, Mars, and so on. This was the Miltonic universe.

At the very bottom of this great circle was hell, the prison-house of the lost, below what might be called, for clear description, the antarctic circle ; the earth and the planets, between this and the equator. And from the time of the resurrection of Christ,—the first one to enter heaven,—the saints went straight up to the empyrean, and the sinners went straight down to hell.

I said that Milton lived and wrote his poem in this transition time ; and it was not long after his poem was published before the whole Ptolemaic universe, as Dante and Milton both conceived it, passed away from the belief even of the common people, though certain ideas and phrases connected with that Ptolemaic

universe survive even to the present time. We
familiarly say that the sun and moon rise and
set, although we know that they do nothing of
the kind. This merely to suggest to you that
there are large numbers of phrases connected
with the Ptolemaic universe that are in common use to-day. We have changed the meaning. We understand that they are not to be
taken literally ; and yet we continue to use
them.

It was a process of hundreds of years, the
passing away of the Ptolemaic universe from
the common beliefs and thoughts of men and
the taking the place of it of the Copernican
universe in which we know we are living to-
day. These spheres dissolved, melted away
into infinite space, into measureless ether.
We learned that there was no up and no down
in the universe except as related to the particular planet on which the thinker or speaker
might find himself at home. I remember
when I was a little boy—and I refer to my
own personal feelings and thoughts because
they are probably paralleled by the thoughts
and feelings of so many other people—that I
used to look up to the planets and stars by
night, and think, how glorious, how brilliant,
it must be up there! I had not waked up to

the consciousness of the thought that I was
even then as much " up there " as the dweller
on any possible sun or planet.   You remember
that beautiful verse of Thomas Hood,—

> " I remember, I remember
>   The fir-trees dark and high ;
> I used to think their slender tops
>   Were close against the sky ;
> It was a childish ignorance,
>   But now 'tis little joy
> To know I 'm farther off from heaven
>   Than when I was a boy."

But Hood might well be comforted.   He
was not any farther off from heaven ; and
we are not any farther off from heaven ; even
while on our commonly called dull, sin-cursed
planet ; for the earth is a planet, glittering,
shining in the eyes of the dwellers of any
other of the heavenly bodies who may be near
enough to see it.

We are in a new universe, then.   The old
earth and the old heavens have passed away.
And, with the change of this philosophical
and scientific theory of things, the theological
world found itself confronted with the problem
as to where they should locate their hell and
their heaven.   We sometimes remember that
the Catholic Church opposed science, that

it had the thumb-screw and the Inquisition for people who asked questions; and it is perfectly true that the decay of the Latin races in Europe to-day has its root in religious persecution. For ages, for generations, every man who dared to think had his head taken off or was tortured to death in some less easy way. For many generations, thinking, having a new idea, was a crime. Under that kind of process how can you expect anything but national decay?

They were confronted, then, I say, with the problem of having somewhere to place their heaven and their hell. They opposed the new science—these Protestants—just as bitterly as did Rome. Old Protestant theologians charged Newton with atheism, when he discovered the law of gravity which accounted for the movements of the heavenly bodies. They said he was taking the stars and the planets out of the hands of God and putting them into the keeping of a law, and so he was atheistic. Ministers to-day ransack the Newtonian theories for illustrations of the magnificence of the power of the Almighty. Down to the time of Kepler, who discovered the great laws of planetary motion, there was no one wise enough to advance a theory to account for the movements of the planets any more rational than that on each one of them dwelt an angel whose business it was to guide it through the sky, as Phaethon drove his chariot across the classic heavens. This was the attitude of Protestants as well as Catholics.

Let us see now where they could locate their hell and their heaven. For a long time the discovery of the rotundity of the earth, and the fact that it moved around the sun, did not disturb these theorisers in the least. They still located hell within the earth; and they found a vivid confirmation of the theory that the earth contained hell in the fact that, the deeper down they dug, the hotter it grew. And they regarded Vesuvius, Ætna, and other mountains that belched forth smoke and flame as being vent-holes of the pit. One minister, an old theologian, more distinguished doubtless for his piety than for his sense of humour or his knowledge of physics, accounted for the re-volution of the earth on its axis by the belief that the centre of the earth was the place where the souls of the damned were impris-oned, and that it was their struggling to climb out of the pit that acted precisely as the struggles of a squirrel on the wheel of his cage acts, and so produced the rotation of the earth on its axis. This is not very ancient ; and doubtless he had a good many devoted followers, even as Brother Jasper, of Richmond, Virginia, has had in our day, who declares, in spite of all the astronomers have to say, that "the sun do move." Any man who vigorously asserts any of these ideas is sure to have a certain kind and class of followers.

After a time, belief in the earth as the abode of the damned was given up ; and some darker planet, supposed to exist somewhere in space, nobody knows where now,—they do not attempt to locate it any longer,—was chosen, where the souls of those who are in torment abide.

They found as much difficulty in locating heaven as they did in locating hell. No longer could they say it was just above the dome of blue, for there is no dome of blue except as an optical effect ; and, as I said, in the present universe there is no up and no down except as related to the centre and the circumference of the earth. That which is up at noon is down at midnight, and *vice versa*. So they could no longer look up, except morally, to the place where God and the angels and the saved were to be found. There has been a great deal of ingenious speculation on this question.

Some theologians have supposed that the surface of our glorious sun was the place of abode of the blessed. Physically, I grant you, so far as we know, it may be possible. Others have looked for the central star in our galaxy, which is the Milky Way. Others have sought still farther for some sun central to the entire physical universe and around which all things revolve. They have thought that that, and that only, was the appropriate place for the throne of the Almighty.

But we are faced by many practically insuperable difficulties in these theories the moment we begin to reason. It has been told how many years it would take a train of cars, if a track could be laid, to travel from the sun to the earth. If it had started in the time of Shakespeare, it would still have a great many years to travel before it reached here. Even if the soul could travel with the speed of light, it would take eight minutes and a half to get to the sun; it would take three years and a half to get to our nearest neighbour beyond the solar system ; and there are suns so far away that we know it takes twenty, thirty, thousand years for light to travel across the intervening space. So, if we should accept any of these central suns that have been imagined as heaven,

it would take the soul so long to get there, even
if it travelled as fast as light, that the friends
who started at the time of Adam would hardly
now have gotten under way.   In that case we
should not be able to speak, if we accept Mr.
Talmage's theories on that subject, of having
any friends at all in heaven ; we might say
that we have some who have started on the
journey, that is all.

You see, then, the difficulty that confronts
one when he attempts to locate either hell or
heaven in the astronomical universe that is
known to us at the present time.   There are
other theories which seem to me more rational.
I shall have occasion to deal with them later,
and so do not dwell on them now,—for instance, that the souls of those who have in-
habited this earth do not leave the vicinity of
our earth at all, except as they wish to travel,
but that the spirit world, good and bad, wraps
round this old planet like an atmosphere.   I
shall speak of this further.

Now I wish to raise another question, as to
who are the inhabitants of these hells and
heavens, according to the teachings of Protestant theology.   The old Catholic father, Tertullian, in a letter to his theological foes, pictures
himself looking down upon the damned, they

presumably among them, and cries out, " How I shall exult, how I shall laugh, when my time comes, and you are there!" Thoughts even more horrible than these you may find in Protestant writers.

Who are they that are to dwell in hell, and how long are they to be there? First, all the heathen. There is no great Protestant creed in Christendom that finds any place for the salvation of the heathen any more than does the Catholic creed,—not one. All the countless millions of them are doomed forever. And to let you have one little side glimpse, so that you may not think this antique, and that I am talking about ideas that are no longer held, let me give you a modern illustration. When I was living in Boston—about four years ago—there was a young man connected with one of the Congregational churches who wished to go as a missionary to Japan. He was examined as to his belief. He did not announce this as a positive opinion, it was simply a question with him,—he wanted to be permitted to think that perhaps, if a man had no possible chance in this world to hear about or accept Christ, he might have one chance at least to hear about him and accept him after death. He promised that he would not preach such a heresy as that.   As an honest man, he simply confessed that the question was lying in his mind, and generating there a doubt as to whether or no he might be permitted thus to believe.   And the board of commissioners, who had in charge the matter of deciding as to whether men should be permitted to go and preach to the heathen, would not appoint him ; he could not go.

That is modern enough ; and the heresy would seem to be mild enough.   None of the heathen, then, to be saved !   And oh, how many times as a boy, when once a month our weekly prayer-meeting was turned into what was called a " missionary concert," have I heard people urged and urged and pleaded with with tears to give money to send missionaries, because countless millions of heathens were dropping ceaselessly into hell !

Who else ?   In the Episcopal Church, unbaptised infants ; in the Presbyterian Church, non-elect infants ; in the old-time New England Puritan Churches, non-elect infants.   These are in hell, as well as all the infants of all the heathen peoples of the world that have been born in all time.   Do you think this is ancient ? It was preached in early New England.   Let me suggest a picture.   It seems brutal to even mention it, because it is so horrible; but people ought to know that these things are still in the creeds. An old sermon pictures God as holding an infant over a burning pit until the flames scorch him, and that infant's turning at last like a viper and spitting its venom in His face. It is perfectly logical, if every child is born in sin and depraved; the difference between an infant and an adult being only the difference between a young rattlesnake and one fully developed, with all the venom, that is all.

These, then, the great majority that have ever been born, are to be in hell; and, if I should dare to picture the kinds of suffering that have been described by ministers in their sermons, you would turn away with your hearts aching and your heads bewildered with the horror of it all.

It is to be for how long? Forever, forever. I remember, in trying to hint how long eternity would be, using this supposition: Suppose a bird were permitted to visit this planet from some other planet once in a thousand years, and carry off one grain of sand. At the end of a thousand years coming and getting another grain. When it had carried off the whole planet, eternity would not even have begun. This is Protestant teaching still. I bid you recall that there is not an authorised creed in Christendom that does not teach it now. There are people, young women, young men, who would not look on voluntarily and see a bug impaled by a naturalist and pinned in his museum, who will join, and support with all their influence and their money, churches that are teaching these infamies against God, because they happen to like the embroidery of an altar cloth, or the music of the choir, or the attitude of the priest when he swings his censer.

What does it mean ? It means either that these people have no hearts or no brains or else that they do not use either of them ; and whoever will may take his choice.

Do you know, by way of contrast, who is to go to heaven ? A few people admitted because they were invincibly ignorant,—this is granted by some of the churches. A few churches admit some of the noble heathen who did the best they knew in the dark of nature. Some are coming to admit all infants, though it is illogical and inconsistent with their creed that they should. As a general thing, it is the elect, or the baptised, or those who partake of the sacraments and are true to the external forms of the Church. These are the ones who are to go to heaven. I will not dwell on that. I wish to come to another point.

What are they to do in these places ? In hell, nothing but suffer. It is utterly purpose-less,—no growth, no progress, no possibility of outcome except to suffer more and more forever. Hell exists to illustrate the supposed justice of God. And the people who go there, according to most of the creeds, are the ones who have been elected to go there (or to be passed by and let alone), not on account of their character or what they have done, but by the pure will of the Almighty.

And what is to be done in heaven ? Nothing, according to the old creeds, except to listen to music and join in it, if you can. No progress there, no growth, no hint that the great astron-omers can pursue their magnificent science, no hint that an artist can either grave or paint, no hint that any of the grand men of the world can carry on their professions,—that the philo-sopher can study and generalise, that people can do anything human.

Notice, for example, an illustration as to how all discussion of this sort is cut off. Mrs. Ward (Elizabeth Stuart Phelps) wrote her book *Gates Ajar;* and if you are as old as I am, and noticed anything about it, you noticed the storm it roused. Why? Because she dared to intimate that somebody had peeped through the gates ajar, and had seen that heaven was not so bad and stupid a place, after all. She said, for example, that the little girl who had hungered and had yearned all her life long for a piano might possibly have a piano. Everybody thought that was horrible. And yet, if you stop and think of it, a piano is not a bit more material than a harp, though it is a little more modern. But the Church has generally been opposed to anything that is modern.

Miss Phelps made heaven a human sort of place, where was a chance for the play of human faculties; and since that day women like Gail Hamilton and other writers have dared to say their say. The old conception of heaven has been reformed in a hundred different directions. It is made more human, more natural; and it is believed that there is play there for the grand human faculties which men really possess and the natural functions which they enjoy.

The churches have always believed,—these old Protestant churches,—not that a person went immediately to the final heaven or the final hell.   There are books written to prove, not only that the soul is detained for a time in an intermediate condition or state, but in an intermediate place as well.   In other words, you will see that the foundation of it is in the doctrine of the resurrection of the body.   People have said that man is only half a man without his body.   As his body has shared in his sins, so it deserves punishment as well as his soul ; his body has shared in his sacrifices and penances, so it ought to share in his rewards. So he cannot reach the final place of bliss or of torture until after the resurrection of the body and the general judgment.   And almost every single one of the creeds of Christendom teaches still the resurrection of the body. They overlook a few objections which are so great as to make it an absolute impossibility. And this is not an old idea.   During a little controversy that went on last year I had some correspondence with an Episcopal clergyman just over the river in a neighbouring city ; and he said that if there is a single Episcopal clergyman that does not believe in the literal resurrection of the body, he has no business to occupy his position.   So this is not entirely an outgrown idea even among those whom we fancy are more or less liberal.

Mr. Talmage, I remember, in one of his grandiloquent rhetorical sermons, gives a vivid description of arms and legs and other parts of the body that have been cut off, sunk at sea, buried on battlefields, or lost in the wilderness of the West, coming flying through the air seeking their mates on the day of the resurrection of the body. And innumerable ministers have taught that only after the resurrection of the body and the joining of it with the soul can there be a complete and finished hell or a complete and finished heaven.

If you raise the question as to whether that could be heaven where people know that father, mother, brothers, and sisters, or friends, are in hell, let me tell you that one of the commonest teachings you will find from Jonathan Edwards, from Martin Luther, down, is that the sight of the tortures of the damned will only increase the felicity of the blessed in heaven.

The Rev. Dr. Momerie, a popular preacher in the Established Church of England, preaching in London for a good many years, and with whom I am acquainted, says he heard a minister preach not long ago, who said, " Do you suppose that the sight of your friends and relatives in hell will interfere with your eternal felicity?"　And his answer was that it would not; for the saved will be so in accord with the thought of the justice of the sinner's punishment that they will even take delight in it. And Jonathan Edwards went so far as to say, that not only would we, on account of our belief in the justice of God, acquiesce in it, but he dared to suggest the infamous thought that happiness was always increased by the sight of an opposite condition.　But Dr. Momerie said that, if these things were so, he would rather go to hell than be in a heaven the inhabitants of which were engaged in such hellish delights. These are the words of a member of the Church of England.

My great objection to the hell of the Protestant churches is its infamy, its opposition, not only to the love of God, but its hideous injustice.　My objection to the heaven is that there is no free play for any faculties which are so human that I could care nothing about it without them.　There can be no growth, no progress, no new learning, no widening out of discovery in the conquest and taking possession of the universe.　I do not say that better thoughts are not coming to be preached.　I do say, however, that the majority of Protestant preaching has been such as I have repre-

sented.   And I do say that the creeds still
stand unchanged, in which these ideas are em-
bedded like fossils in the rocks.

Let us thank God, then, that the old earth
and the old heavens have passed away, and
that a new earth and a new heavens are coming ; and let us look forward with grateful joy
to their advent.

VIII

THE AGNOSTIC REACTION

THERE have been in the world, at more than one stage of its history, classes of people who claimed that they knew almost everything. There have been also—and perhaps at the present time their number is larger than ever before—those who modestly claim that they know almost nothing ; who are proud, perhaps, of taking that humble position. It seems to me that Paul strikes grandly the great middle truth, when he declares that we know, but we know in part only,—when he refers to the fact that, as a child, he thought and felt and understood as a child, but, when he became a man, he put away a whole world of things that he supposed he knew, as a child, and contented himself with the humble statement that he was one of those who knew only in part.

The characteristic of the childhood world is to be governed and swayed almost exclusively by feeling, to accept its beliefs through the heart, by contagion of emotion, rather than as the result of conviction and through the head. The lowest people that you find to-day—the lowest in culture and civilisation—are the most certain of all the people in the world in regard to their beliefs, undisturbed by doubt, accepting that which has been taught them, or which they have got by a certain emotional contagion, without any sort of doubt or question.   And the chances are that they will believe that those people who doubt in any degree are in a hopeless moral and spiritual condition ; that the reason for their doubt is a moral reason ; that, if they were better than they are, had been converted, had passed through a certain spiritual experience, they would see and know that to which now they are blind.   This, I say, is a characteristic of early man, and of men living to-day in conditions similar to those which pervaded the early world.

When we come to what has been called the Middle Ages, and what has also been called at the same time the Age of Faith, what do we find?   These ages may roughly be spoken of as covering the time from the fourth or fifth century on to the culmination of the Roman Catholic rule in the thirteenth or fourteenth century.   What is the characteristic of the people of these ages? They knew almost nothing at all about this world, but they knew everything about the other. This is the most pronounced general characteristic we can discover of these epochs in the history of man.

Let us note, for example, what they knew. They knew the nature and character of God and His condition before the universe came into existence. It has been told by some of them what He was doing, what He was thinking, what He was planning; and fragments of this kind of knowledge you will find in nearly all the early and well-established creeds. They knew that at a certain period in eternity God waked up and decided to create something. He created the angels, created heaven,—this first. They knew why He did it. They knew that, after a very brief period, there was a rebellion among these angels, and that a certain part of them was cast out into the abyss; and then suddenly hell came into existence as an abode for them. They knew that after that, God decided to create what we call the world, —the universe, as we see it, which was not in existence before,—and that He created man and placed him in a certain beautiful garden. They knew that man fell, and why he fell, and when he fell. Some of them carry this knowledge to such a minute extent as to tell us the day of the week on which the work of the creation was finished, or on which the fall took place.

Then they thought, after the fall, that man was cast out of this beautiful garden, and started this epoch of labour, of disease, of moral evil, of suffering of every kind. They knew that there was an age-long battle going on between the unseen spirits of good on the one hand and the unseen spirits of evil on the other, and that the object and crown of this battle was the possession of the human soul ; that they were raging against each other, one that they might deface God's fair human creation, the other that they might protect, beautify, and glorify it.

They knew what was going on in heaven among the blessed, what was going on among the damned. They knew that both waited for the last day of judgment and the resurrection of the body, and that then everything was to be fixed in a final condition forever and ever. These things they knew all about. They did not, however, know enough about this earth that they were living on to know whether it was a flat plain, or a cube, or a sphere. They knew that nobody lived anywhere except on the top of it. Why? Because of a certain old Hebrew book which spoke about men's living on the face of the earth. And they knew also enough—or supposed they did—to know that it was impossible for men to walk with their feet up and their heads down. There could consequently be no people living on the other side of the earth.

You see, then, that this was the condition of things during the Middle Ages. Men knew all about the other world. Strangely enough, they knew almost nothing about this. And how had they come into possession of this knowledge? Greece had been studying science, had been philosophising, had been making herself famous in art. Rome had developed a great literature, and established laws and an order of government which the world has been imitating ever since. But, suddenly, the progress of Greece and Rome came to an end. No more Greek philosophy, no more Greek art, no more Greek science, no more Greek studying of the natural facts of the world. But for the happening of one thing there is no good reason to suppose that this development of Greek knowledge and Greek investigation, Greek science, Greek art, might not have kept on until now.

What happened ?   One thing on the part of the leaders of Christianity happened, and that one thing put a stop for fifteen hundred years to the intellectual advance of mankind.   What was this one thing ?   The early Church made the enormous mistake of accepting the idea that certain old books of law and history and poetry and legend and tradition, which had come into its hands from the Jews, constituted an infallible, divine revelation, that told the world all that the world needed to know, both about this earth and about the unseen.   And its reverence for these books as infallible and inspired made it wicked to ask questions or to study.   So that for a thousand or fifteen hundred years the intellectual advance of the world, in regard to this intellectual outside knowledge, practically came to an end.

I do not mean that intellectual culture, thinking, developing the subtlety of the human brain, the power to think, came to an end.   By no manner of means.   I believe that in what we to-day call, in comparison, the Dark Ages, the candle of the human intelligence was still kept burning.   Only, do you not see, its investigations were confined within certain narrow dogmatic limits ?   An artist was at liberty to paint ; but the only patron he could find to buy or use the results of his genius was the Church, and he must paint traditional Church scenes and ideas. He might philosophise as much as he pleased,—on the wings of speculation fly to the uttermost limits of his power to think at all; but, note you, when he got through with his flight, he perforce, at the peril of his life, must come back and settle down within the limits of ecclesiastical dogma. He might study science, investigate the nature of the earth, the nature and history of man. He might study astronomy, study any region of the universe that was accessible to him; but, if he wished to live and keep on in his scientific investigations, again he must come back and settle down quietly within the limits of ecclesiastical dogma. He might think what he pleased. If he wished to live, he must not write, publish, or speak anything not endorsed by the ecclesiastical domination that ruled the world.

This was the condition of things. Do you wonder that they were dark ages, that it took man a long time to be willing to be burned, or lose his head, or be imprisoned for life for speaking one of his thoughts, for daring to communicate to somebody else his innermost ideas ? A man dared not speak to his most intimate friend; for this friend might be under bonds to the Inquisition, and be obliged, as he believed, on peril of his immortal soul, to reveal what was whispered to him in the privacy of intimate friendly conversation. This was the condition of the Church for centuries, the condition of the intellectual, artistic world.

But by and by there came a change,—that change which, using the French word which first came to have this meaning, has been called the Renaissance. Following Matthew Arnold's example, who said that the word had become so thoroughly at home among us that it ought to be anglicised, we call it the Renascence : it was the rebirth of man. And what started it? It was the discovery afresh of and the growth of a new interest in the classics,—the writings of Horace, of Virgil, of Homer, of Plato, of Aristotle, the great philosophers, scientists, thinkers, poets of Greece and Rome. Those who had become familiar with these great classics learned that the Greeks had been engaged in the study of nature, and that the kind of world they were beginning to discover was not the kind that had been outlined in the Hebrew Scriptures, which had limited their study. The artists waked up to the idea that this world was beautiful, and that it was not the kind of world described in these old writings. They began to notice that the human body, that of man or woman, was beautiful, — the most beautiful thing on earth, infinitely more beautiful than the grief-smitten, emaciated, haggard form of the Christ, as traditionally represented, or of the saints, which had formed the staple subject of the artistic work of the preceding ages.

Philosophers began to think, stimulated by Aristotle and Plato. They began to philosophise about the universe and about human history and about the Church, and found themselves face to face with imminent danger. They could not agree with the dogmas of the Church; and they could not speak except on peril of their lives. Now and then was found a man like Galileo, who had not the stuff in him to wish to be martyred, and so would kneel in the presence of the priests and pronounce a recantation, whispering under his breath as he rose, however, his own belief that the world did move. Now and then you will find a man like Giordano Bruno, who was so impressed with the truth that took hold of him, that he must write, must speak, and yet who would flee from country to country, attempting to save his life, until at last, being trapped and being too honest to lie, would suffer himself to be burned at the stake.

These were the characteristics of the period
of the Renaissance. Men began to think, to
study. It was a rediscovery of this world;
and it was a profound and growing doubt as
to whether the Church knew so much as she
claimed to know. Out of this experience,
what have come to be called Modern Science
and Agnosticism at last were born. What is
the characteristic of modern science? It is a
demand for evidence before belief; it is asking
for proof; it is saying what seems to most of
us to-day mere common sense. Why should
I place myself—body, heart, soul, brain—in the
keeping of a claimant who either cannot or
will not bring me any good credentials on
which to base the claim to take possession
of me?

It seems to us to-day—it certainly seems to
me—the very last reach of impudence, of im-
pertinence. Why should I give my brain,
body, heart, soul, into the keeping of an institution—I care not how old—that cannot give
me a reason for taking possession of me that
appeals to the first instincts of intelligence or
common sense? Time enough that the scientific spirit and the scientific demand for at least
a little bit of evidence should come into the
world.

The Church said, "You must take all these things on faith." And let me suggest to you here that I wish you would study carefully the meaning of the word "faith." There is not a more abused word on the face of the earth than the word "faith." That which the Church ordinarily calls faith is the sheerest credulity. Take the position of the old Father, Tertullian, whose sweet words I have quoted to you, about exulting and rejoicing on seeing his opponents by and by in the flames of hell. What did he say about belief ? *Credo, quia impossibile est.* ("I believe, *because* it is impossible.") And he thought it a pious thing to say. The only thing that I know of to match the stupidity and insolence of a saying like that is the parody or parallel of it made by a little boy in Sunday-school, when somebody asked him what faith was. He said it was believing something that you knew was n't true.

And the Church carried this matter so far as to make it a virtue,—note, I say it with perfect carefulness and weighing the responsibility of my words,—a virtue to lie. An English bishop within this present century has said that a man would better lie—*i. e*, deny his doubts and his real belief—than utter beliefs which would disturb the faith of the members of the Church.   It may be a virtue to lie; but, if it is, I am going to practise a vicious course. I cannot lie, though all the churches on the face of the earth tell me it is God's will that I should.   I will appear before the throne at the last day, and say: " O God, even if what they told me was Thy command, I refused to lie; and I appeal to Thee as to whether or no I was right."   I will take my chance of eternal hell on that issue.

What has been declared to be faith?   Accepting any statement which the Church wanted you to hold without reasoning or against reasoning.   Now that condemns Paul's definition.   I will accept the well-known New Testament definition of faith, translating it a little more freely and in modern phrase.   The author of the Epistle to the Hebrews says that faith is the underlying substance of things hoped for, the persuasion of the reality of things not seen or not yet seen.   That is in perfect accord with science.   Darwin, Huxley, Herbert Spencer, all accepted Paul's definition of faith; and they practised it, too, every week of their lives.   I heard Huxley lecture in Chickering Hall, when he was here; and he showed a splendid example of such faith.   He

traced the ancestry of the horse, and said that
a certain number of the horse's ancestors had
already been discovered, and that, if the next
one ever was found, it would possess such and
such characteristics, describing what sort of an
animal it would be. He had hardly been in
Europe six months before Professor Marsh of
Yale discovered this animal's remains in Col-
orado; and they matched perfectly what Huxley said that they would. There was faith in
the working of God in nature,—the faith that
God would not deny Himself, that He worked
according to certain laws and methods.

Another illustration of faith: I may say I
have faith in a man with whom I have been acquainted for twenty years. I do not believe he
would lie or steal or commit a burglary. If
he is accused of one of these, and I am asked
if I think he is guilty, I say, No. Did I see
it done? No. Did I know anything about
it? No; but I know the man, and believe in
him. That is faith; but faith, you see, not
made out of nothing. It is faith based on a
long intimacy and experience, based on facts
and speaking out of facts. But if a man is
accused of committing a crime,—a stranger
whom I never saw before,—and I should say I
had faith in him and believed he was innocent,

I should be talking nonsense. I should have
no reason for having faith in him.

So there is a certain class of facts that come
under the name of religion to which faith applies, and another large class to which faith
has no relation whatsoever. Suppose I should
say, I have faith that a certain man was born
in Nazareth a certain number of years ago,
and up to thirty years of age followed such a
course of life ; that after that time he spoke
certain things and did certain things,—suppose
I should talk of faith in such facts. I should
be talking nonsense. Why? Because the
biography of any man, what he said and what
he did, are matters of history,—matters for
critical, scientific investigation. They are not
matters to accept in the lump,—by opening
your mouth and shutting your eyes, by "having
faith." To do that is not faith ; it is sheer
credulity. But there are great spiritual truths
which are not dependent on history and criticism, that are such as come under the range of
what is called faith. Some day I may treat the
matter in a fuller and larger way.

But the result of the coming into the world
of the scientific spirit after the Renaissance,
and the development of Agnosticism, was a
very practical one. Before I go into detail

as to what these results were, I must give you a definition of Agnosticism; for it is a word that did not exist until Mr. Huxley invented it, although it has gone into all the dictionaries and become very common now. He belonged, at a certain period of his life, to a metaphysical club, or society, that represented all sorts of philosophical and religious beliefs. The members all had names except himself. One was called a Pantheist, another a Christian, another a Theist, another a Metaphysician; but he was without a name. He said it made him feel something like the famous fox after he had left an important part of him in a trap: he did not look like the rest of his friends, and did not feel at home with them. Their various names ended with an "ist," or were connected with some sort of scheme called an "ism." And it occurred to him to take the name of "Agnostic," and feel at home with the rest. And the meaning of it was, "I do not know." In the early days of Christianity, men were sometimes called Gnostics, from the Greek *gnosis*, which means knowledge; the Gnostics were the people who knew. This Gnostic philosophy was not a scientific philosophy at all. They did not know on the basis of any evidence. If you had been acquainted with them, you would have found that they had evolved from their inner consciousness the most of the knowledge they had; but they felt that they knew,—knew the invisible, knew truth, knew spiritual realities.

Mr. Huxley, in his humility, took the name " Agnostic," which means one who does not know; for he said, while all those around him knew so much about all sorts of things, he could not say that he did. Why? Because he kept the word " knowledge " for its real use. Let me say to you, with all the force and frankness that I can put into the phrase, " You have no right to say that you know anything, unless, on the one hand, it is a fundamental truth of consciousness, or unless you have proved it, and demonstrated by adequate evidence that it is true. When most people say "I know," they will be found if you catechise them a little, to *believe* a thing with a good deal of force. But a person has no right to say he *knows*, unless he does know. I have tried for years to keep the words " know " and " knowledge " for those things. There are a thousand things that I believe, that I do not know. There are a thousand things that I think, for which the evidence seems strong enough to be called probable;

there is more in its favour than there is in favour of the opposite proposition ; but I do not know these things, I simply believe them probable. I hold them tentatively ; and I wait for evidence.

Now there is the essence of Agnosticism, as Huxley meant it. He said : "You tell me about a certain kind of God,—a kind of God who foreordained everything that was to happen in this world, and who is going to damn people who do not believe in a particular Church. You say you know it. I don't know it. As to this I am an Agnostic." "They tell me this Bible is infallible from one end to the other," Huxley might say. "I do not know anything about it; and I think I can prove the contrary. But if you will not accept evidence, I cannot have anything further to do with you, because I cannot talk with a man who will not hear evidence." So as to this whole range of so-called spiritual things, the existence of purgatory and hell and the traditional kind of heaven, Mr. Huxley said simply, "I don't know." No true Agnostic ever says he knows a negative can be proved any more than can a positive. He may feel very strongly about it either way, like other men.

There is a certain class of men who call

themselves Agnostics to-day who do not re-present the true idea of Agnosticism at all. They may have different canons of proof, they may have personal bias and prejudice, so that you could not convince them with any amount of evidence that a certain thing is true, merely because they do not like it, and they do not want it to be true. Now that kind of a man is not an Agnostic at all according to the definition of the man who invented the term; he is simply a bigot. For you need to remember in all these discussions that there are scientific and philosophic bigots, just as great bigots as the most bigoted theoologian that ever lived in the history of the world. I know men who, if you should offer them evidence in a certain direction, would, in a lordly fashion, with a wave of the hand, sweep it out of existence. They will not go two steps to see whether you have any evidence or not. That is bigotry. It is not Agnosticism, it is not science. So there may be Agnostic bigotry as well as Presbyterian bigotry or Baptist bigotry.

The real Agnostic is a truth-seeker. I have never found one in my life who wanted to doubt anything that a man with a heart would not wish were untrue. I have had men say to me, with tears in their voices as well as in their eyes, that they would give their lives to know that there is another life after this. One of the noblest men living in this city to-day, as once we were sitting talking together, and the long hand on the clock began to near the figure twelve, where the short hand already was, said to me: "Mr. Savage, if I could have as much evidence, personal to myself, of a continued life after death as you have had, for the price of it I would gladly die when that hand reaches twelve."

I have never found any of these men who were sneering at the beautiful faiths of the Church, who were sneering at the real Jesus, who were sneering at God, who were sneering at the hope of a future life. They simply reject, and are rejoiced that the evidence is not sufficient to compel them to accept, the things that are inherited from the hideous barbarism of man half-way out of the animal, —that is all. They do not want to believe in a horrible God; and I do not. They do not want to believe in a horrible hell for good people, simply because they had not a little water put on their heads by a priest who was a hundred miles away when they were dying. They do not want to believe in a heaven where people are going to sit on clouds and sing hymns forever. They do not want to believe in any future pictured in the old creeds.

I have been corresponding with one of the most famous of these men in the world; and he is longing with heart-break for evidence that is satisfactory to him for a belief in the kind of God that I believe in. He is longing for a belief in something that will enable him to look death in the face without any fear. He is longing for the continuance of human love and human relations. He is longing for belief in everything that is dear and tender and true. Constituted as he is, and having studied as he has, the evidence that is commonly offered, he says, is not enough to convince him. And so he has to say, reluctantly: "*Agnosco* [I do not know]. I wish I did; but, to tell the truth, I do not."

And if there is any God in this universe who is going to damn him for saying he does not know, because that is the truth, I would not enter His heaven, if I had the chance offered me, to sit beside the highest ecclesiastic in the world who would be mean enough to condemn him.

This is the reaction of Agnosticism that we

are in the midst of to-day, and such the men who are more or less Agnostic; and, if you only knew, you would find them in many of the pulpits of New York. If you only knew, you would find them sitting in front pews, and gladly paying the bills, because they think that possibly the Church is doing some good, at least morally and philanthropically, for humanity. If you only knew, you would find that the men to whom this word applies are often the noblest men, the most upright men, the farthest off from being liars, the most honest in their business, faithful and loving and true, and doubting because the evidence to them is not sufficient, and because they feel that they must be honest with themselves and tell the truth, or else, if there is another life, they would not be worth saving.

These are the men who are labelled by those who guess at their opinions "Agnostics." If that is what Agnosticism means, I am an Agnostic myself, and want all the world, that cares, to know it. I do believe, however, that there are more certainties in the world than these doubters are aware of, and that as soon as they can be made manifest to them they will gratefully accept them; and I believe that we are on the verge of discovering and

making manifest the grandest beliefs of the
ages, so that we can set them down with their
evidence in the presence of these honest
Agnostics, and have them thank us from the
bottom of their hearts for enabling them to say
at last, " I know."
12

IX

THE SPIRITUALISTIC REACTION

IN the fifteenth chapter of the First Epistle to the churches in Corinth, the fourteenth verse, it is written, "If Christ be not risen, then is our preaching vain, and your faith is also vain."

Of course, from the point of view that Paul occupied, if Jesus had not come up from the underworld and been seen alive, then their faith, that Christians were to be delivered from death, was vain, and their preaching without any adequate foundation. As most of you doubtless know, the Easter hope and the Easter celebration, under some name, in some form, are thousands of years older than Christianity. But the significance of our Christian Easter lies in this one fact, to which I call your special attention. The whole meaning of it is here,—the belief that a man, whatever else or more he may have been, after he had passed through the experience called death, had been seen, had communicated with his friends, and so demonstrated that death was not the end of conscious existence. This is the significance of Easter; and this precisely is the significance that is claimed for Spiritualism.

The believers in this great faith tell us that they, too, have had communications from those who have passed through the experience called death; that they have been seen; that their voices have been heard. Mark you, for the present I am saying nothing whatever as to the truth of this claim. I wish to call your attention emphatically to the fact that the significance of the Easter claim and of the claim of Spiritualism are precisely the same; and, if they are true, they demonstrate the same great truth and fill the human heart with the same great hope.

A Spiritualist would very likely tell you that the advantage was on his side, because the evidence, whatever it may be, which is offered to us for the fact eighteen or nineteen hundred years ago, is old,—the witnesses cannot be cross-questioned; it must be taken on faith: while the advocates of Spiritualism will show you that their facts are present, happening almost every day in the year, accessible to anybody; and they offer them to you only on the basis of the scientific claim that evidence can be shown. This is their claim ; and it is a claim that we shall find of great significance as we pass on to the development of our theme.

I have been showing you in preceding chapters, how the almost universal belief in life beyond death has been held, and has grown, in all religions, among all people. I have shown you, especially, during the last two or three chapters, how this belief has come to overshadow the world, so that the common lives of common men have been lives of other-worldliness, so to speak,—the present life has been diminished and belittled in the comparison, until it has seemed of almost no moment. I have shown you how this over-belief, that offered very little in the way of scientific evidence, that offered no present or modern facts in its support, has been reacted against by the spirit of inquiry, of question, of modern science, until there is, at the present time, on the part of the more intelligent classes of the people, and those who have come to accept the method of science as the one and only method of knowledge, very serious doubt concerning these dear, precious things of the human heart that cannot, as yet, be demonstrated,—so far as the general opinion is concerned.

I want you to note that we are to deal in this chapter with a reaction against a reaction. Though it has been proved to the satisfaction of those who have been dealing with the great material facts of the universe that the existence of the soul and its continuance after death are incapable of proof, the great masses of the people—who love, and to whom human life is as nothing without love—have refused to accept the verdicts of science—have refused to believe that those men who have said, " I do not know," have probed the matter to the bottom.   They have said : " We cannot give up the trust and the hope ; and athough we admit in a general way, and with regard to all other themes, the supremacy of the scientific method, yet we must believe here or we cannot live." And so, in spite of the methods and the claims of science, the great majority of the common people have clung to this hope, and believed that somehow and sometime it would be vindicated as a rational hope.

It is interesting to notice the attitude of the poets as indicating this great common belief and trust.   For instance, the first verse of this hymn by Whittier :

> " Oh, sometimes comes to soul and sense
> A feeling which is evidence

> That very near about us lies
> The realm of spirit mysteries."

I have had the pleasure of talking this whole matter over with Mr. Whittier, and know that he believed the essence, the substance, of what is called Spiritualism, though he did not give much of his time to what is called investigation of the facts.   But he cries out, you remember, showing how close it was to his heart:

> " Alas for him who never sees.
>   The stars shine through his cypress-trees,
>
> .   .   .   .
>
> Who hath not learned in hours of faith
>   The truth to flesh and sense unknown,
> That life is ever Lord of death,
>   And love can never lose its own."

And, then, you are familiar with those sweet words by Longfellow:

> " There is no death ! What seems so is transition.
>   This life of mortal breath
> Is but the suburb of the life Elysian,
>   Whose portal we call death."

I could quote to you passages from hundreds of poets,—from Sill, who has written so finely under the title of *A Morning Thought*, to Browning, who believed in immortality with his whole soul, so that he defied death, and said that he was not one to be afraid when death came ; he did not wish to be delivered from any of its pictured horrors, he did not shrink from feeling "*the fog in his throat*"; he did not fear to face death in any form, and under the title of *Apparent Failure*, another poem, he asserts his great eternal hope for the poor wrecks of humanity, washed by the waves of crime to the horrible strand of the Paris morgue.   Browning is not very orthodox in his faith ; but he believes in God and the human soul to such an extent that he thinks they never can be finally separated.

And, then, there is Tennyson's lovely *Crossing the Bar*, closing with the words :

" For though from out our bourne of Time and Place
    The flood may bear me far,
  I hope to see my Pilot face to face
    When I have crossed the bar."

Then there is a beautiful little poem by Aldrich, written after the death of his intimate friend, Bayard Taylor.   I must give you just a line or two :

    " When the soft
Spring gales are blowing over Cedarcroft,
Whitening the hawthorn ; when the violets bloom
Along the Brandywine, and overhead
The sky is blue as Italy's,—he will come,
Ay, he will come !   I cannot make him dead."

And I would like to repeat to you two passages from Walt Whitman. I will quote one brief one. I love to say this in all presences in his honor, since he was a man so misunderstood. I do not know of more than two other men in the history of this world who are like him in this respect,—and one of those is Jesus, and the other Socrates,—who so magnificently, so calmly, so conqueringly met death. I know of nothing in all literature to match the sweet, grand things which Whitman has written about death. This one you can place beside Tennyson's *Crossing the Bar :*

> " Joy, shipmate, joy !
> (Pleased to my soul at death I cry,)
> Our life is closed, our life begins ;
> The long, long anchorage we leave,
> The ship is clear at last, she leaps !
> She swiftly courses from the shore ;
> Joy ! shipmate,. joy ! "

That was Whitman's welcome to death. Note also the grand challenge of Holmes :

> " Is this the whole sad story of creation,
>   Told by its breathing myriads o'er and o'er,—
> One glimpse of day, then black annihilation,
>   A sunlit passage to a sunless shore ?
>
> " Give back our faith, ye mystery-soiving lynxes,
>   Robe us once more in heaven-aspiring creeds !

Better was dreaming Egypt with her sphinxes,
The stony convent with its cross and beads."

The poets, then, I say, who have, almost universally,—with exceptions like Omar Kháy-yám, the author of the *Rubáiyát*, and Byron,—touched the human heart, have sung of hope and life, not of despair and death.   And yet—and here is the meaning of the point I suggested a moment ago—these men, and all modern men, have felt the touch of this great question that has swept over modern life, that has challenged them to bring their proofs or else surrender their beliefs.   And the one wonderful thing about Spiritualism, without any reference to its truth or its falsity, is what I called your attention to a moment ago,—it does not ask your blind belief.   It says, Come and see, and do not believe a word beyond what you can see or hear or feel of reality that carries with it this great conviction.

Now let us look at a few of the characteristics of Spiritualism.   It has filled libraries of discussion.   What is called modern Spiritualism, as I suppose all of you know, began in Hydesville, a little town in New York State, in 1848. It had been preceded, however, in the modern world by other facts, which were given a similar interpretation.   The family of the Wesleys, of which John and Charles were the most distinguished members, was turned topsy-turvy by what were supposed to be visitations from the unseen world, though they were not accepted as from above, but rather taken to be devices of devils. Perhaps the most of you know that the home of old Dr. Phelps in Connecticut was haunted by similar happenings. Professor Phelps of Andover, the son of the old Doctor, held the belief firmly to the last hour of his life that they had a spiritual origin, though his orthodoxy prevented him from consenting to any but a demonic explanation of the visitations. Professor Phelps, as you know, was the father of Mrs. Elizabeth Stuart Phelps Ward, who has written so many books dealing with themes of this character. This preceded the outbreak at Hydesville. And what did this consist of? Of rappings, of movement of physical objects, of all sorts of communications. I am taking now the theory of the believer, so as to save the trouble of circumlocution. It accounted for all sorts of happenings for which they could find no explanation but a spiritual one. Of course, the cry of fraud was raised, of devils' work; but here and there were found some to accept the belief that these things were genuine communications from the other life.

I wish to consider the attitude of the ordinary church towards this movement and similar ones.

It has always seemed to me a little curious that the average minister will tell you that you are a very wicked person if you doubt immortality; and he will tell you, with equal emphasis, that you are a very wicked person if you undertake to prove it. He wants you to accept it as an article of faith. And this for a moment must be a reminiscent time for me. I understand the attitude of these men, because I have lived through it. Long before I attempted to study the matter at all, I knew all about it. I preached against it. I demolished the entire movement conclusively. I believed that it was false, foolish, wicked. I proved everything, just as a young minister is apt to do before he has studied matters. I demolished Theodore Parker in the same way before I had read one of his books. I have noticed generally that the thoroughness with which any one of these causes is demolished coincides with the ignorance of the demolisher. That has been the result of my research and experience.

At any rate, the ministers opposed it. And yet it has always been a wonder to me that they should not have welcomed it. The Catholic Church has been wiser. It has admitted that there have been what are commonly called "miracles" all the way down, accepts them to-day, and has said to the Protestants,—and the Protestants have had no answer: It is very strange that God should appear to teach and guide His people in one age of the world, and should leave them without any teaching or guidance ever after.

I have wondered why ministers should not welcome demonstration, at least for the sake of those who without demonstration could not accept this central principle of Christianity. But I have wondered whether the truth might not be hinted at by certain experiences which I have had myself.   I have had what purported to be hundreds of messages from the other side ; and I have never had a single one that was soundly orthodox. Wherever Spiritualism has gone, whatever else it may have done, it has liberalised the thought of the people who have accepted it, in regard to God's dealing with this world.

But there is one thing no church can afford to overlook.   There has never been a religion on the face of the earth that did not start with precisely the same kind of occurrences that the

Spiritualists claim are taking place to-day,—
never one. Christianity started with what?
With appearances of people from the other
side, with voices out of the unseen, with apparitions and strange happenings. Judaism
was born out of the same kind of atmosphere
and supposed occurrences. So was Buddhism,
so was Mohammedanism, so has been every
religion that I have been able to study in all
my long life of research. All religions claim
to have had at their beginning visions and
voices, appearances, teachings, coming out of
the unseen. Only it is immensely to the advantage of Spiritualism, let me repeat again,
that the occurrences are supposed to take
place to-day, the witnesses are alive, can be
cross-examined. You can find out whether
they are honest men or dishonest men, whether
or no they have been deluded or have really
found out something of value. You can find
out these facts to-day; while concerning the
basis of all the other religions you must simply
take the questions at issue on faith, because
they are no longer open to investigation. In
regard to most of them there is not a single
first-hand witness to any of these strange occurrences. The only first-hand witness that
we have to the seeing of Jesus after his death

is Paul; and Paul does not claim to have seen him in the body which was buried in the tomb. He saw him in a vision on the road to Damascus.

Now I wish, finding myself continually misunderstood and misrepresented, to state one or two things concerning my own personal attitude. I read a paper some years ago at Saratoga before the National Conference on *Immortality and Modern Thought*. I was not a little interested and amused after the meeting to find that many of my good friends, who hated Spiritualism, had gone out saying, " Dr. Savage has lost his head, and gone over to the Spiritualists." And there were many Spiritualists there who went out of the meeting angry and disgusted because I was not a believer, or at any rate did not dare to say so. On one side they were angry because I had seemed to be for it, and on the other side because my attitude seemed against it. My conclusion was that probably I had hit the middle path of truth and soberness.

I have never called myself a Spiritualist. I have been charged with being a coward and time-server for not doing so. I believe that at the heart of Spiritualism there is a great truth, perhaps not yet clearly outlined, understood, or demonstrated ; but I have never been able to call myself a Spiritualist, because, as that word is used popularly in the newspapers, it would utterly misrepresent me.   There are so many things connected with the movement that I not only do not believe, but with which I am disgusted beyond words, that I am not willing yet to wear the name.   I hardly need say that it is not cowardice.   If I have never proved anything else in the last thirty years, I think I have proved to those who are acquainted with me that I am not afraid to wear any label which belongs to me.

Spiritualism as organised has been its own worst enemy.   There have been a large class among Spiritualists who are so credulous that, no matter what sort of a story you tell them, they will simply ask for a bigger one.   I have quoted in a preceding passage Tertullian, the old Church Father who said he believed "because it was impossible."   This comes very near the attitude of a great many Spiritualists I have met.   They will believe anything, no matter what, that is told them, without investigating or asking for evidence.

Another thing that has been against them— not with me, however, I take pride in saying— is that the movement started with the poor

and the meek and lowly ones of earth; but
there is a striking parallelism right in there
with early Christianity.   You know people
went around then, not asking whether or no
Jesus was a real prophet or if what he said
was true, but how many of the scribes or the
Pharisees believed on him.   Men commonly
wait for a popular movement before they join.

Spiritualism started in this same way; and
I have met a great many people who have
confessed to me privately that they believed,
but would not say so because it was not
popular.   One famous English scientific man
told me in private conversation that he had
been experimenting for years, and knew that
Spiritualism was true; but, he added, "I don't
talk with people about it; because I used to
call every man who had anything to do with it
a fool, and I don't enjoy being called a fool."
So he kept still.   This is the attitude people
have taken in regard to it; and to-day you can
never get at the number of Spiritualists by the
census.   I venture to believe that you cannot take a stand on any spot on Manhattan
Island and throw a stone without there being
somewhere within the radius of its fall one or
more families who are studying Spiritualism
privately in their own houses, and who are

believers, but dare not let their next-door neighbours know it for fear of ridicule. I have had people, when I was travelling, sit down beside me, and evidently feel their way. They would ask a question or make a statement just to try me, to see whether I was going to be unsympathetic. The moment they found I was sympathetic, they would tell me wonderful things within the range of their own experience. So the country is full of people who have had strange things happen to them, and who believe, or at least wonder if there is not "something in it."

One of the worst enemies of Spiritualism is the dishonest practitioner, the "fake medium," or the people who cover him up through any personal favour, or, as they mistakenly think, for the honour of the cause and to save it from disgrace. If there is any man on the face of this earth meaner, more utterly contemptible than any other man, it is he who will take money, coined from the broken hearts, from the hopeless tears of those who long to know whether or no their dead are alive ; and take it, not even for what they believe to be a genuine message from the other side, but simply for the sake of the money. When a person will do that, I do not believe there is anything on the face of the wide earth too mean for him to do.

These are some of the obstacles that have stood in the way of the progress of the movement called Spiritualism.

Now one word in its favour, so far as it goes. I have said that I do not call myself a Spiritualist. I shall announce to you frankly, later on, what I believe and where I stand. There are certain things that ought to be said in defence of Spiritualism. At one time all the newspapers in New York had long articles as to the belief of the Rev. Dr. Abbott, of Plymouth Church ; and they were coupled with an account concerning the belief of Dr. Hillis, his successor, both of whom believed, according to their own statement, all that is essential to Spiritualism, only they were both very careful and most anxious to guard themselves against the possible suspicion of belief in such vulgar things as a rap on a table or a movement of a physical object. Frankly, I can never understand what there is so foolish or degrading in a rap. Suppose you were in one room of a hotel and I in another, and I should want to call on you. If I am courteous and half-polite, I do not open the door and rush in without finding out whether you want to see me or not. I tap on the door to announce myself. Suppose I have a friend in the Unseen, close by me, who wishes to communicate something to me, and finds he can call my attention by a tap. Is there anything so very silly about it? If there is, I am too dull to discover it.

And, then, as to this question of the movement of physical bodies. Did you ever think, —please stop and consider this, for it is the essence of the whole matter,—if there is a power in the universe that is capable of lifting a grain of wheat or a hair without the use of any muscular or physical effort, then he who has discovered this has crossed the Rubicon and has answered the question as to whether this universe is material or spiritual. If a particle of matter can be moved without muscular contact or physical force, in the ordinary sense in which these words are used, then it is demonstrated to all the world that there is unseen spiritual power at work there ; and, if these movements indicate intelligence, then the power that moves is an intelligent power.

And yet people talk about these things as though they had no significance at all. This is the shallowest way of dealing with the matter. I have had it said to me a thousand times that whatever claims to come from the other

side is always silly and foolish, nothing digni-
fied, nothing worthy. That, again, shows that
the person who makes the statement is not acquainted with the facts. I have had what purported to be hundreds of messages come from
the other side, and many have asked me what
kind of messages they were. I have frequently
replied that they were very much on the level
of my daily mail. I get some very silly things
every morning in my mail, some malicious
things, some stupid things. I get some things
tender and noble and sweet, some things full
of intelligence. And, if we could once get
our heads free from the nonsense inherited
from the old and discarded ideas of the past,
—such as the idea that the moment a man dies
he is either a devil or an angel,—this is just
what we should expect. If I should die on
the platform of my church, and come to consciousness in five minutes, I should expect to
be neither more foolish nor more wise than I
am now. Why should I be? And, if I should
send you a message, why should it not be on
the average of my present intelligence?

The very silliest thing on the face of the
earth, it seems to me, that people do, is to go
to mediums for advice, particularly in regard
to financial matters. I am fairly "up" in arith-

metic; but I should hope no one of sense would come to me, if he could, after I was dead, about stocks on Wall Street.   I do not know why I should be supposed to know so much about a thousand things because I am dead.   Fools die every moment; and I suppose they are as big fools five minutes afterwards as they were before.   If I wanted advice in financial matters, I would rather have a word from Pierpont Morgan than from a congress of a thousand spirits, although I knew the message genuine.

This by way of a hint that you can elaborate in a hundred directions, and see how silly it is to go to " business mediums," as they advertise themselves.

To recur to this question of intelligence that purports to come from the other side, let me say this; find out whether or no the people who make this claim know what they are talking about.   There is much trash that purports to come as communicated from the other world.   At the same time there is a whole library of the noblest moral and spiritual teaching that I am acquainted with.   I know one book, for example, the author of which was an Oxford graduate, who during a large part of his life was connected with the

School Board of the city of London, a member of the Church of England when he began, and afterwards a clergyman in that Church, who became a Spiritualist and a medium. His book was written automatically, as he tells us, through his own hand. Sometimes in order to divert his thoughts from what he was writing, he would sit and read Plato in the original Greek, while his hand was at work on its own account. And this book, contrary to what people ordinarily believe, went squarely against his own religious creeds, and converted him before he got through; and it contains some of the noblest ethical and spiritual teachings to be found in any Bible in all the world.

So do not trust the first squib that you come across in the newspapers in regard to the character of the communications or what happens on these occasions : just do a little inquiring on your own account. The newspapers are not always infallible in regard to all these matters.

The ethics of Spiritualism, as published by its best representatives, are as high and fine as you can find connected with any religion on the face of the earth. This does not prove its peculiar claims at all; but it does prove that it is not a movement to be treated with utter scorn and contempt, or as being connected with the off-scouring of the earth.   Early Christianity, you remember, if you will read over the writings of Paul, was made up of the people that the respectable did not have anything to do with.   Spiritualism has until modern times been made up of much the same class of people.   But now such names as Mrs. Elizabeth Barrett Browning, Lloyd Garrison, and others by the score are associated with it ; and some of the noblest, most intelligent people with whose names you are familiar were open and avowed adherents of Spiritualism.

Remember, then, that this is a great and, in the main, genuine, sincere movement, and that, whether its claims or any part of them shall ever be found true or not, it stands for the same great hope that makes the glory of Easter morning.

X

THE WORLD'S CONDITION AND NEEDS AS TO BELIEF IN IMMORTALITY

I NOW propose to consider the present condition of thought, of belief, in regard to immortality, in so far as my experience, my correspondence, my years of acquaintance, have led me to think or know, and then to point out what seem to me some imperative needs for certainty, provided certainty can be attained. If there be no certainty, why, then, we must stumble on as best we may.

In the first place, I wish to note that nobody questions that the evidence on which, as Christians, we accept our faith in immortality is old, is far away, is waning in its power over the popular mind. One of my critics in a newspaper has said that to question the evidence for the resurrection, the reappearance of Jesus, would take away the reason for belief in the existence of all the famous Greeks and Romans. It seemed to me that he was not particularly wise in making such criticism. If my eternal salvation depended on my belief in the existence of Cicero or the accuracy of some reported saying of Socrates, then there would be a parallel between that criticism and the actual situation. It would become a burning question for all men earnestly to discuss as to whether or no Cicero did live, as to whether or no Socrates did speak certain words. But now suppose somebody should prove that Cicero was a myth, and his orations were delivered—as some one once humourously said—by another man of the same name, what difference does it make to us? Suppose nobody can get at the precise verbal accuracy of a single one of Plato's writings, except for the sake of our literary regret, who cares? Nobody's soul, nobody's future, nobody's heaven or hell, depends on any of these questions. So that, when anybody suggests a parallel between the one case and the other, he is talking either without seriousness or without good sense.

It becomes a matter of great importance to us to know whether or not we have good evidence coming down from eighteen hundred years ago that somebody who had been called dead had been seen alive. And yet, as I have said, we have only one first-hand witness to any such things' having ever occurred ; and that witness testifies that he never saw Christ in the body in his life, but saw him only in a vision on the road to Damascus.

The testimony, then, is old ; the witnesses cannot be cross-questioned. We do not know who wrote Matthew, or who wrote Luke or Mark or John. We know nothing of the authorship of any New Testament book,— nothing certain, I mean,—with the exception of a few of the epistles ascribed to Paul. No wonder, then, as these facts of knowledge become common property among the people, that there grows a question, a doubt, as to some of these great things that have been taken on the testimony, the tradition, of the Church.

You remember the old fable of the Hindus; how the earth rested on an elephant, the elephant on a tortoise, the tortoise on something else, and so on down. As we go up the stream of human tradition, we find that one man says that somebody else said a certain thing, and somebody else said the same thing to him, and some one else to him, until at last we can find nobody at all who saw or heard anything at first hand. All scholars know this. What wonder, then, that doubt at last permeates the Church itself, and that Christians begin to wish that they might come somewhat nearer knowing,—knowing that one thing which is nearer to the heart of the world's misery or happiness than anything else that can be conceived. The attitude of great masses in the Church is perhaps best set forth by these saddest, tenderest words that Lowell ever wrote :

> "Yes, faith is a goodly anchor ;
>   When skies are sweet as a psalm,
> At the bows it lolls so stalwart,
>   In bluff, broad-shouldered calm.
>   .   .   .   .   .   .
> "But after the shipwreck, tell me
>   What help in its iron thews,
> Still true to the broken hawser,
>   Deep down among seaweed and ooze ?
>
> "Then better one spar of Memory,
>   One broken plank of the Past,
> That our human heart may cling to,
>   Though hopeless of shore at last !
>
> "To the spirit its splendid conjectures,
>   To the flesh its sweet despair,
> Its tears o'er the thin-worn locket,
>   With its anguish of deathless hair.
>
> "Immortal ! I feel it and know it :
>   Who doubts it of such as she ?
> But in that is the pang's very secret,—
>   Immortal away from me."

Is not this really the condition of thousands, in churches where they think they believe and have been taught that they believed from childhood? I had a letter some time since from a woman down in Maine, whom I have never seen. She was a young woman, married four or five years ; and her husband was a physician. He was fond of fishing, and was one day drowned ; and she was left alone. She writes me a strange, sad letter. I shall not give it to you : it is too private, too sacred ; but it dripped with tears of utter despair. She had been a member of an orthodox church all her life : she said she had supposed she believed ; but suddenly the hawser had broken, and she was afloat under skies with no sunshine. And, curiously enough, to show the drift of public opinion, she says : " I write to you because you are not of my Church. If I should go to my minister, he would feel obliged to tell me what the Church teaches. I write to you because I know you are tied to nothing but your opinion of what is true ; and you will tell me just what you think." And she pleaded with me to tell her if I really believed in God, if I really believed in any future life.

This is a hint of what I have found in many

sad cases. I find that people are taught that they believe; and they believe that they believe until the stress comes, and then everything is adrift. Not only the people in the pews. I am accused sometimes of accusing my brethren : I do not mean to. I know that the worst thing that I am doing is to talk a little "out of school." Perhaps I ought not to do that. But let me give you one illustration of the condition of things in the pulpit. There was a minister, who is not living now, whose name was a household word in almost every home in America,—a minister supposed to be in the main orthodox, at any rate as orthodox as Dr. Abbott. I preached once in the city in which he lived on a week-day evening, when he was free; and he was in the audience. When we got through, he walked down the aisle with me, and said, "I agree with every single word that you have spoken to-night," and then added, with a touch of genuine pathos in his voice, "only I wish I felt as sure about the future as you seem to." Two or three days later I had a private talk with him in his own home; and he, a Christian minister with a Christian following, with all the Christian traditions behind him, the Bible in his hands, said to me quietly and privately,

"Mr. Savage, for the first time in my life you have given me at least *some* evidence of a future life."

There is this great sweep of doubt over Christendom. The faith is an old tradition, weakening as the years go by; and it is not strong enough to make people glad and brave in the face of death. Paul, as I have told you, could meet death with a shout of triumph. Who does it now? Who says, It is better to die and be with Christ? Do we not shroud our homes, our bodies, and our hearses in the blackest of dismal black, as showing how little we truly hope in life beyond the grave?

I have told you already the position the Agnostics have come to assume. They do not want to disbelieve in God or a future life; but they have come to believe that honesty compels them to say that they know what they do know and do not know what they do not know, —that is, to tell the truth, and they tell it with brave hearts, though their lips quiver, not because they are in love with doubt.

Then there is a certain sect—small, I think, as the civilised world is searched—of out-and-out materialistic atheists. Not merely doubters, but men who think it is demonstrated that there is no soul or spirit, and that there is no God, and, therefore, no future.

I corresponded a few years ago with one of the then most famous men, Dr. Maudsley, the author of a large number of powerful and weighty books, in which he deals with what he regards as science. In one of his letters he writes, a little humourously, though the humour was somewhat grim :

"Why, Mr. Savage, as I look over the world and see, not the kind of people that we create as ideals, but people as they really are, all the way from bushmen and tramps clear up to the common kind of millionaire, I cannot make it seem worth while on the part of the universe to keep them."

He said it seemed to him that it was the worst kind of economy to perpetuate such creatures through all the coming time. I had but one answer to give him. I suggested in my next letter that it seemed to me barely possible that some of the millionaires, as well as some of the tramps, might have germs of possibility within them that would some day come to something really worth while to keep. That is the foundation stone of evolution; and I really think it is a more sensible position than the Doctor's, though he never confessed to me whether he agreed with me or not.

Then there are thousands and thousands of men who are simply afloat, adrift. They do not know where they are nor what they believe. They have gained a smattering of modern science. They are suspicious of religious tradition. And they are so many that, as Mr. Moody says, out of about seventy millions of inhabitants in this country there are no more than thirty millions who ever go to any kind of church. I am not at all sure that this is true. I hope it is not. I give it on Mr. Moody's authority only. But, if it is, half the people in the world no longer care enough about the great sacred traditions and issues of religion to ever step inside a church ; and it is a most terrible indictment against the Church, —more, I think, than against the people who stay away.

If people get nothing in a church but super-annuated and dried-up dogma, absurdities, things that they would not call common sense five minutes after they had left the church door-way, why should they go to church ? Why should you take the trouble three times a day to gather from all over the town, wherever you may be, and sit around a table called a dinner-table, if there is nothing on it to eat or nothing for which you have any sort of relish ?

It may be, then, the fault of the Church, if these statistics be true.

But there are thousands of these men who do not talk about it. As one famous old minister said once, when a young, zealous enthusiast tried to get him to talk, and, failing, burst out with, "Have you no religion at all?" "None to *speak of*," was the reply. So there are thousands of people who do not unbosom themselves; they do not stop the first man they meet on the street, and tell him that they really doubt whether they shall ever see the wife who died the week before or the child that was taken away in the night. These doubts exist; but people are chary of speaking of them. Let me give you an illustration of the kind of talk that comes out when a man feels perfectly free. I have an old friend who lives in another city. I have known him for more than twenty years. We met in Paris. I had not seen him to speak with for some years. I knew he had a pew in an Episcopal church, that his wife was a devout believer and a constant attendant. I knew from past experience with him that his religious faith was not particularly strong. He said to me:

"Dr. Savage, here I am walking on a plank; and it reaches out into the fog, and I have got to keep walking.

I can see only ten feet ahead of me, possibly. I know that pretty soon I must walk over the end of that plank, —perhaps to-night, perhaps next year, perhaps in twenty years. I don't know when; and, when I walk over it, I have n't the slightest idea into what, and I don't believe anybody else knows. And," he added, " I don't like it."

If you could get at the secret heart of thousands of the noblest and best men of our modern civilised time, you would find that they occupy a position very similar to this.

Here is this great, wide-spread doubt, then, eating into the Church, teaching materialistic philosophy, threatening to darken the skies of the Agnostic, taking the heart and hope out of the noblest men and women ; while the great majority—if you press them with the question as to whether they know—will tell you, if they are frank, that they do not.

Now, if this is a condition that cannot be helped, why, the best we can do is to be as well reconciled to it as possible, forget it as long as we can, and let the matter go. But I cannot understand the thought, or lack of thought, of the thousands of people who act as though it were not worth considering, or are not ready to turn their hands over to decide the question one way or the other. For, in my judgment, there is no other question on the face of the earth for one moment comparable to it in importance. As Professor Hyslop of Columbia once said, we put thousands of dollars into an expedition to dredge some deep sea or to explore the pole, to see if we can discover at last its ice-locked secret. We are spending thousands—we that have them—in all sorts of expeditions and explorations; and yet these same men never stop to appreciate for one moment the reality that right here, within our own bosoms and brains, is an ice-locked pole and a Darkest Africa more inaccessible to most than any spot on the round globe, and about which the wisest men know almost nothing.

Let us now consider for a moment. It seems to me that it is exceedingly important for us, if possible, to decide as to whether we are animals, without souls, or are souls, wearing our animal bodies; for, as I love to say a thousand times over, I do not believe for a minute that I have a soul. If I have, I might lose it, as the theologians say. I believe I am a soul, and have a body.

But the great question to be decided first of all in this whole realm is to find out for a certainty—not as a matter of belief, as I have just put it—whether or no it can be demonstrated that I am a soul. Can we prove yet that thought is not as much a product of the brain as bile is of the liver? That is what some of the materialistic philosophers ask; and they say that we have not yet proved the contrary. That is the point. Am I a soul? If I am, then, at the least, I am a far different kind of being from what I should be if I were only a body,—a temporary machine for grinding out thoughts which are to cease when the machine gets tired. In other words, I can never know myself until I know whether I am a soul or not. There are certain numbers of men who, with the grand quality of Matthew Arnold, can say :

> " Is there no other life ?
> Pitch this one high."

But the great majority of men are more likely to say with Paul, if we have no other life, " let us eat and drink ; for to-morrow we die." That is the common philosophy about it.

I need to know, next, whether or no I am a soul, not only for the sake of finding out what sort of being I am, but in order to place in their relative positions of importance the great interests, ambitions, pursuits, of humanity. If

I am an animal only, a thinking machine, the machine and the thought both destined to end after a little time, why, then it makes a great deal of difference in the value to me of political or social position, of money, of fame, of friends, of selfish indulgence in certain things I happen to care for. If I am a soul, then all the great mountain heights, the lofty peaks of the world, from my high position of observation are levelled out and down, the valleys are lifted up and the mountain peaks are made plain, as it was prophesied they would be to those who occupy this position.

But if I am only a body, with a few bodily tastes for a few years, to satisfy, you may preach to me as much as you please; but I am not going to live the same kind of life that I would find natural and reasonable if I were a soul. What is the use of self-sacrifice, of self-denial, for fifty or sixty years, when all that is to come of it in any case is for the whole to go under the sod and be forgotten, neither God nor man nor angels to remember or to care? Will you tell me why on that philosophy of life I should sacrifice myself and suffer overmuch? My happiness and comfort are at least as important as those of anybody else. Why should one person on that theory sacrifice a moment's peace for the sake of a similar moment's peace for somebody else?   There is no outcome, no object, in it all; for the peace of both sacrificed and sacrificer goes into dust, and that is the end.

The decision of this question, when it comes, is going to make a great difference with our political theories and practices.   In the Middle Ages there was a spiritual power that was able to lift the humble and to put down the high.   In those days any poorest peasant might become the triple-crowned pope, at whose feet all spiritual authorities lower than he must bow in humility.   You remember an illustration which I will use for my purpose, because it is familiar to you all,—how Cardinal Richelieu, the weak, trembling old man, drew an imaginary line about his niece Julia, and cried to the king and his courtiers:

> "Then wakes the power which in the age of iron
>   Burst forth to curb the great and raise the low.
>   Mark where she stands! around her form I draw
>   The awful circle of our solemn Church!
>   Set but a foot within that holy ground,
>   And on thy head—yea, though it wore a crown—
>   I launch the curse of Rome!"

And the king trembled in the presence of the paralytic old man, and fell on his knees in fear.

There was a power then that could come to the defence of manhood and humble the mighty ; but we are in a democratic age now. Nobody cares very much for the pope except those who are nearest to him. I have heard good, devout Catholics in this country talk in this way. They say : It is all very well for the pope to manage spiritual affairs ; but, when he dictates to me as to where I shall send my child to school or how I shall vote, then I am done with him. This indicates the coming of a new spirit into the Church. Old spiritual power then is waning ; and we need a power to take its place, if there be one possible,—a power that shall make men feel the awful responsibility of being men, and make them feel that not at some future time only, but day by day, they stand at the awful judgment-seat of the Almighty and Omniscient God, and that the universe is against them if they are against the right. We need a doctrine that shall teach men this in politics ; we need it in society.

If we are not souls, but only bodies, those of us that happen to be rich and able to deck and array our bodies, and command the un-questioning obedience of the great masses of the people, are free. We have nothing in the future to fear. We will take the grandeur and

the greatness of it as we go along; and we
will use the rabble for our behoof. This has
been the attitude of men so situated. But let
the doctrine be not only taught, but believed
by rich and poor ; let it be known to be God's
truth, that each man is a son of God, each
woman a daughter of God ; that the little time
that we are spending here below is but a
moment in our eternity ; that we are making
ourselves by our characters, and that the
eternal future hangs, hinges, and turns on
character and truth and right, and not on
power and frippery and the display of wealth,
and do you not see the different kind of world
that would be the result ?·

Then take it industrially. I have a friend
who has spent years abroad studying the
industrial conditions. Fortunately, he is
financially situated so that he can go where he
pleases and stay as long as he pleases, and
meet the men in office, the men who labor and
study, and converse with the authors of books
on the subject, and become perfectly familiar
with the situation. He said to me four or five
years ago that he considered the settlement of
this question as to whether we are souls or
merely bodies as more important to the settlement of our industrial problems than any and

all other considerations whatsoever. For he said: Go to Germany, study the masses of people in Europe, and they say: It used to be the nobility and the Church; they had it all their own way: they told us to be content in the position in which Providence has been pleased to place us; postpone to another world our reward. Now, he says, it is not the nobility; they are beginning to break down: it is the *bourgeoisie* and the Church, the comfortable middle classes and the Church; and they still tell us that we must be humble and content in the place in which it has pleased Providence to place us. But they say: We have studied science, we have read Huxley and Darwin and Herbert Spencer; and we do not believe any longer in your bugaboo God or Devil. We doubt whether there is any future life, and we do not propose any longer to be put off to the future for our share of the comforts of living. And when the great teeming and seething millions come to hold a creed like that, why, all the institutions of society, its sacredness, its cathedrals, its colleges, its universities, its nobility, its great men, will be only flotsam and jetsam on the tide of a flood such as never has been dreamed of before.

For the sake of social order, of industrial

satisfaction and peace, then, men need to be taught,—no lies, mind you; they need to be taught that they are souls, and that how they live, what kind of lives they live, whether or no they cultivate mind and conscience and heart and become noble men and women, are things a great deal more important than the kind of houses they live in or the things that the Gentiles, in the words of Jesus, are accustomed to seek after.

Then there is another class of people—I must speak of these briefly—that need to know.   I can give you the point of view that I wish you to occupy better by telling you of a specific case that came under my pastoral care. A lovely, noble woman, not a member of my own society, came to me one day, and said:

"I would like to tell you about my nephews, Mr. Savage; I am at my wits' end. I do not know what to do.   Here are my two nephews, whom I have loved since they were little boys; and they are growing wild and unmanageable, throwing away their manhood, dissipating their characters, and I find I have no sort of influence over them.   They said to me the other day: 'Why, Auntie, what is the use of talking? We have read Darwin, we know a little something about evolution,'—this was their reading of it,

with which I do not agree, as you know—‘ we
don't believe any more of that flimsy nonsense
about a future life. You can't scare us any
more by talking about the devil and hell and
God's anger. We have gone beyond that.
And we are rich,—we have all the money
we want or expect ever to want. Now, we
propose to do just as we please. We are
going to indulge in all sorts of things that we
desire; and you know perfectly well that there
is n't a family in the city that would n't be glad
to have us marry into it, in spite of their knowing all about what we do. Now, what is the
use of talking?'" And she said, "How can
I answer them?"

My reply was: There is but one answer. If I
could look into the faces of those young men,
and say, I know, and I can make you know by
scientific demonstration that you are going to
live; that you have got to live whether you
want to or not, and that as you cross the border
line you take with you what you are, your own
mean, selfish, warped, contemptible selves,—
if you have made yourselves such,—and that
there is not a moment's peace for you in all
eternity until you come into harmony with the
eternal peace of God,—if I could say that to
them, it seems to me that we would have in our

hands the mightiest ethical power of which the world ever dreamed. We could transform the world.

Two other things I must hint in a word. Would it not be worth while to be certain, for the sake of the comfort and peace that it would bring to our hearts? I know people who do not talk very freely about these things until they get very well acquainted with each other. But I have had people, after knowing them for years, break out, and say: We do not know anything about it; and nobody does. It is a horribly unpleasant subject. Do not let us speak of it. I have tried to push it out of my sight and keep it out of my consciousness. I know that it must come; but do not let us speak of it. That is the attitude of thousands of people—as Paul said, " Through fear of death all their lifetime subject to bondage."

Now, if it were possible to prove that beyond this life is another, that death is simply a gateway that lets us out into a larger and nobler existence,—if we could just know that, would not it be worth while for the sake of the comfort and happiness it would bring to the great majority of men? I do not say it is possible yet to know it. *If* so, would it not be worth while?

And, then, here is that father,—it seems almost cruel to speak of this,—compelled by business to be in another city overnight, returning in the morning to find three children and wife gone forever from his sight and touch, unless this hope of ours be true. All of us have friends, who have passed into the unseen. It is no very great amount of comfort to me to think of them as having gone into utter nothingness, and that I am following them there; for people talk foolishly about this kind of death as being a rest. How can that be rest of which nobody is or ever can be conscious? There is no rest about it. It is simply fooling ourselves with words,— abusing the dictionary. Would it not be worth the study of years to know, if it be possible, that we shall see our friends again and shall know them, and that we shall resume the companionships that have been dearer to us than life here? Why, if this could be once known, the earth would never again be draped in black, the skies could never again weep with rain, every wind would be an anthem and every morning the dawn of an eternal day.

XI

PROBABILITIES WHICH FALL SHORT OF DEMONSTRATION

IN the seventh verse of the third chapter of Titus appears the phrase: " The hope of eternal life."

If you think I am somewhat negative as I start out, you will see that my entire purpose is positive and reconstructive as I get towards the end. Though this theme does not take us quite far enough, it does, I think, take us close to the borderland of that which is real and eternal. Oliver Wendell Holmes once said that, if any one wished not to come into contact with liberal thought in this modern world, if he did not wish to have any doubts of his old-time and traditional ideas, then he must keep away from the common atmosphere of the world; he must let the newspapers, the magazines, the reviews alone; he must stop reading and stop thinking; he must shut himself away from the common light of heaven; for these things are in all the air.

If that could be said by Dr. Holmes concerning ordinary liberal ideas, much more can it be said concerning this great question of a future life. Blessed, say I, are they who are disturbed by no doubts, whose old-time traditions, whose sweet memories of what mother taught, the echoes of the services in the old-time meeting-houses, are sufficient. Blessed, I say, are these; for they escape a good deal of the torture, the suffering, that comes of doubt and question, which doubt and question, however, are absolutely forced upon those who think, in the world of to-day. There is no escaping them, they are in all the air; and you can keep your childhood faith untouched only by keeping away from contact with people who think and ask questions. And yet it is possible that the self-culture wrought out by the doubt and study is worth while.

The number of persons in the civilised world to-day who have more or less questioning about continued personal conscious existence after death, is unspeakably greater than it was a century ago, and beyond any dispute the number is increasing; and it is increasing just in the most important part of this human life of ours. It is increasing among the thinkers, the readers, those who are becoming of such a state of mind that they must have proof before they can quite accept any proposition.

Some of the probabilities, the propositions that have heretofore been urged as arguments in favour of a future life, but which are not scientific demonstration, we are now to consider.

When I was contemplating this special subject I wrote a very large number of letters, a good many to Unitarian ministers, a good many to ministers of other faiths, a good many to laymen ; and in these letters I asked two questions : First, Do you believe in a conscious personal existence after death ? Second, Why do you believe in it ? I wanted to find out, so far as possible, the basis on which this belief rests in the minds of some of the higher and better thinkers of the land.

To my great astonishment, I found several ministers who were not at all certain of it in their own minds ; who had grave and serious doubts as to whether or no there was any conscious personal existence for themselves or for anybody else after death. And beyond this what did I find ? I found only two, or possibly three, persons out of all those to whom I wrote, who gave me what, if I were a doubter and were seeking for scientific proof, would be one single particle of evidence. From only two or three did I get anything that I should count evidence in the scientific sense of the word. And I had to feel, as the pressure had been growing on me for years, that it was time somebody made a serious, careful study in this direction to see if there could be found anything solid enough on which to put a foot and find it hold. This is the secret of my interest in a year-long investigation in this direction.

Now let us glance at a few of the arguments that you meet, or suggestions that you find, in books, in poems, in sermons,—everywhere; and I grant you they are beautiful, and I grant you they are strong probabilities. They pile up, they accumulate, a hope of immortality. But let us see if we can prove it.

Take, for example, the whole line of analogies that people are constantly following between the dying and the reviving of the vegetable life of the earth. Mrs. Whitney has sung very sweetly:

" God does not send strange flowers every year:
    When the fresh winds blow o'er the pleasant places,
    The same fair flowers lift up the same fair faces,
  The violet is here."

And there is a suggestion in that verse of the continuance of identity through the death

15

of the violet and its reappearance in the coming spring. But the moment you examine it, you see it is only a beautiful illusion. The violet is here, but it is not at all the same violet that was here last year; and in all the æons of earth the same flower has never reappeared. It is no argument whatever, then, that my friend who was here last year is going to re-appear in his personal identity to me after the winter we call death. It is a suggestion, a beautiful suggestion; but there is not the slightest particle of what science demands as proof anywhere about it.

Take, again, these intuitions that are so strong in our hearts, the feelings we cherish. We say we know certain things intuitively; and that feeling used to be a very strong one to me, until Herbert Spencer, and writers like him, came along, and took away the evidential value of these intuitions, by what was, at least, a very plausible scientific explanation of them. They said : " These intuitions are only the in-herited results of the thoughts and the feelings and the fears and the hopes of the human race through countless centuries of the past." I am not sure that Herbert Spencer is right. Un-fortunately, however, I am not sure that he is not right. Consequently, I cannot offer one of these intuitional feelings to a man who doubts continued existence and demands evidence of me. He says that is not evidence; and I am obliged to confess that what he says is true.

Then there are thousands of people—I have come in contact with a good many of them—who are satisfied with saying: I am conscious of immortal life. I am conscious that I am immortal; I feel it, I know it. The magnificent, brave hero, Theodore Parker, was one of the men who held that position. But, not abating a whit my admiration for Theodore Parker, I can but disagree with him at every point here. It seems to me that we cheat ourselves with a misuse of language. What Theodore Parker really meant, and what all people who speak in that way must mean in the ordinary use of the English language, is that they feel very sure, perhaps sure enough for them, as sure as they care to feel. They do not mean to be troubled either by doubt or evidence; and they have a perfect right not to be, if that is their feeling. But I submit to you it is a misuse of language for a man to say that he is conscious to-day of a possible future fact. The question as to whether or no I am immortal is a question as to whether I am going to keep on living after the fact we call death or not. And, since that is a fact to be known, to be realised, to be conscious of only when it comes, —to-night or to-morrow or next year or after forty years,—it is simply impossible that a man should be conscious of it now. So again it seems to me that is not quite enough.

There is another point, one side of which perhaps will be entirely new to you and may startle you at first. In most of the letters which I have received this last year, the great argument as it was put was simply like this: " I believe in God. Therefore, I believe in a conscious personal existence. I do not believe He has created me for nothing. I do not believe He is going to throw away His own handi-work." That does not satisfy me. I do not believe there is a man on the face of the earth to-day who believes more thoroughly, from the crown of his head to the sole of his foot, in God than I do; but my belief, my faith, my trust, is not proof, is not demonstration that God either needs me or is going to keep me after a hundred years. I do not know whether He wants me in a thousand years or not. How can I know ?

But now I am going to turn the thing right around. And here is a matter which, perhaps, will surprise you. If I were a confirmed atheist, if I believed that there was no God in the universe at all, I should still be just as earnestly and eagerly investigating the question of the immortal life. People seem to assume, the atheists all seem to assume, that, when they have got rid of God, they have also got rid of the question as to whether or no there can be any future life. I cannot see for an instant why this force, this nature, this machine, this magnificent aggregation, whatever you choose to call it,—whether there is any God in it or not, —which has brought me here, has brought all of us here, and has put into our hearts all the love and into our brains all the thought and question, has given us consciences, has made us recognise questions of right and wrong, cannot keep me going forever. For, if a force, a universe with God left out, can do all that has been done, I do not see why it cannot also continue my existence through what is called death. I do not see any negative there that is in the slightest degree a necessity.

So, as I said, I should still be studying the question of continued existence if I believed in no God at all. Belief in God does not seem to me proof of a future life ; neither does disbelief in Him seem to me disbelief in a future life. I want, at any rate, something beyond either of these.

Then there is one of the grandest arguments that has ever been used, and one that touches us more deeply than almost anything else; and that is the feeling on the part of noble souls that, as things appear to be so unrighteous and so unequal here, there must be a time and place somewhere when " accounts will be squared "; when the ignorant will have a chance to learn ; when the poor and despised will have an opportunity to develop perhaps the sweet and beautiful life that has had no opportunity here. This has been put forth as one of the strongest of all arguments in favour of the future life.

I remember in one place Theodore Parker said that, when he looked upon the pinched, starved face and hungry eyes of a little boy in the slums, he wanted no stronger argument that somewhere in the universe that boy would have a chance. But, unfortunately for the scientific value of an argument like this, I have seen it turned right around. Books have been written in which it is turned right around. If God does not care anything about the little boy in the slums to-day, and does not see that he gets any chance or any justice, how do you happen to know that He cares for him at all or ever will care for him? That is the way a great many people argue. They say: How do you happen to feel sure that the God who seems to neglect this world, and does not care anything about it, is suddenly going to be very careful and see that everyone gets his rights in some other world? So you see that, at least, when a man flings that in your face, it is not always perfectly easy to answer him.

I believe, myself, it is a tremendous probability in favour of the future life; but, when a man comes to me, and says: I think it is a tremendous probability against the justice of God right here and now, I need to go further than reasserting my original opinion, before I can satisfy him or do away with his opposition.

Then there are lives that never seem to be treated justly here; not only crime prosperous and rich, and spattering its mud on our poorer clothes as it sweeps along the avenue,—not only this, which has been a problem to every thoughtful man in all ages,—but there are lives which we know are never finished. They have infinite possibilities in them that have had no chance here to unfold; and it does seem as though God would, God must, sometime, somewhere, give these people a chance. Let me quote to you just a few words from Victor Hugo :

For half a century I have been writing my thoughts in prose, verse, history, philosophy, drama, romance, satire, ode, song. I have tried all ; but I feel I have not said the thousandth part of what is in me. When I go down to the grave, I can say, like so many others, " I have finished my day's work " ; but I cannot say I have finished my life. My day's work will begin again the next morning. The tomb is not a blind alley : it is a thoroughfare, it closes in the twilight to open with the dawn.

But let me anticipate enough right here to say that this was not the prime reason for Hugo's belief. Hugo had been a searcher for years in the realm of psychic phenomena, and had come to feel that the matter for him had been demonstrated. This was known to all his friends, so that this—beautiful outburst as it is—is not the principal proof that Hugo would have given you in conversation. But it is a tremendous probability.

Among the many beautiful letters that I have received during my experience is one from a widowed mother, who is practically left to a lonely life, and who writes : " I long so much to have this matter proved. It seems to me the one theme of any importance. My husband died ten years ago and my life stopped ten years ago.   It seems to me as though there must be somewhere a time and place where this broken life can begin again."

And so I suppose all of us say.   You never yet saw an author who had written what he regarded as the grandest thing he intended to write ; you never saw a painter or a sculptor who did not look upon all his attempts as suggestions merely of what he might do, if only he had the time and chance.   Every person who ever wrote a book has dreamed a hundred more beautiful than ever he succeeded in getting on paper ; and, if the universe is just, if the universe cares, if it means something, it does seem as though there would be a chance for some of these things to be finished sometime, somewhere.

I feel, as I look upon any man or woman with noble qualities of brain and heart, and see him or her nearing the line of the silence, as though I were looking upon a ship a hundred miles from the sea.   I feel as though he or she was not built for simply that ; it suggests to me an ocean sweeping round a planet, with the infinite winds in the sails and the infinite stars overhead.   So this to my mind is a tremendous probability.   I look upon a child as I look upon a little plant in a hothouse.   I know that, if this plant grows, it must be either taken out-of-doors or else it will burst through the roof; it has in it potentialities greater than the hothouse which contains it for a time. So I feel concerning every human soul I come in contact with,—there must be some larger place than this, some grander place for these magnificent possibilities to come to blossom and fruitage. It is a tremendous probability in favour of another life; but I do not quite *know*.

I see a beautiful oak beginning to grow, reaching a height of ten feet. If it has a chance and time, it will grow to be a hundred; and its branches will spread their shade for many yards in every direction. An accident comes: the little oak is knocked over and torn from its roots; and I know that is the end of it. That oak is never again to have any chance to complete itself; and when I grow humble, I find myself wondering why I cherish the conceit that a Power that can create souls by the million should feel under any special necessity of going back after I have been run over to pick me up and reinstate just me. While it is a magnificent probability, it is not demonstration; and I want something more. I am not sure that in my lifetime I shall ever get what all will accept as demonstration. I want it ; and I cannot understand the state of mind and heart of anyone who does not want it.

I come now to a point which seems to me a probability stronger than any I have touched upon.   I have shown in the course of sermons which I have preached that there never has been a time on the face of the earth in any religion when the majority of the people did not believe that they were going to live after the fact called death.   The age-long and universal fact of this belief is the thing I would have you consider for a moment.   If there is no reason in it, no basis for it, no realisation of such a promise, why should the universe from the very beginning lie to its child, man ?   Why fool us with such a promise ?   Why bend down over us with its beautiful sky and clouds and the whisper of the winds and the music of the brooks, and whisper to us ever,

" There is no death.   What seems so is transition " ?

If it is not true, how does it happen that the universe in all ages should have been saying, " It is true," to the heart of man?   It seems to me that we may consider ourselves in a sort of fashion as standing related to the universe about us as a coin is related to a die.   You pick up a clean, fresh twenty-dollar gold piece, and examine it ; and you feel perfectly certain that for every mark you find on the gold piece there will be something corresponding in the die. Have we not a right to feel that we as men and women are the products of this universe in some such real sense as that ; so that whatever you find universal in all the lives that have ever been, in all the hearts that have ever felt, and in all the brains that have ever thought,—you feel that here is something which corresponds to the die, a reality in the universe that pressed upon and shaped us to what we are ?

It seems to me that this is one of the most magnificent arguments with which I am familiar ; and yet somebody might tell me that Nature, in most cases from the beginning of the world, has been telling us things that were not quite true, that we have had to correct Nature's impressions from the very beginning, finding out generally that they were wrong. Some extreme doubter might meet us with a point like this ; and we should at least be a little discouraged, and wish we had something stronger to say.

Then there is still one more argument, and this,—let us say it in spite of all the scepticism and agnosticism that have come out of modern science,—however we may be impressed by the worldly tradition, the materialistic tendencies and qualities of modern science, this is a gift of science,—and what is it ?—the death of materialism. The Church from the very beginning has hurled her anathemas and thundered her anger against materialism ; but the Church from the very beginning until to-day has never seriously hurt it. Materialism has lived and flourished as intelligence flourished, grown as knowledge grew, until in these modern days it threatens to overcome the world. But the scientific men themselves have carried their studies so far as to learn that they cannot explain the universe and man on the theory of materialism : and so you will find a man like Huxley facing every fact, ready to give up anything that he could not prove, and even saying that it was immoral to hold beliefs that could not be proved scientifically,—and I am inclined to agree with him,—we find a man like Huxley, who says, " If I am compelled to choose between the materialism of a man like Büchner," whom I have quoted as saying that thought was a product of the brain, just as bile was a product of the liver, " and the idealism of Berkeley," who believed, as Christian

Science teaches to-day, that all material things are mere temporary illusion, " I should have to agree with Berkeley." This is where science has come. He does not, by the way, agree with either of them : neither do I. But materialism as an accepted theory of the universe is killed ; it is no longer correct science nor good philosophy. No man who holds any high rank in the scientific world to-day believes that thought is a product merely of the molecular movements of the brain. Tyndall, who came as near being a materialist as any famous man of modern times, said that though there was always a correspondence between the molecular movements of the brain and the thought that accompanied those movements, yet the gulf of separation between them was just as impassable to-day as it was in the savage periods of the history of the world. And when you have proved beyond question that mind, feeling, love,—these things,—are infinitely more than planets, than stars ; that they rule the world, are the mightiest powers on the face of the earth ; you have gone a good way towards proving that they can get along without matter ; but, unfortunately again, simply that demonstration does not prove continued existence.

I may know that mind is more than matter ;

that my brain, that can measure the sun, is unspeakably grander than any sun that shines in the depths of space. I may know that that sun will cease to exist. How? Cease to exist as a sun. But there is not a single particle of its matter, not a particle of its accompanying force, that is going to cease to exist. So I may prove that my mind is mightier than the sun, and prove that mind, or its elements, will exist uncounted ages; but that does not prove, I must confess, that conscious personal existence of this same mind is going to continue for ever.

Half the human race, nearly, believes to-day that mind is everything and matter is illusion; and yet, at the same time, it universally denies the conscious personal existence of the soul. So that the two do not necessarily go together, and believing one is not quite enough to prove the other.

Now, I have one point more with which to tax your patience, and this is more impressive, to my thinking, than any of the others with which I have yet dealt; and it is the drama of this universe,—how it started, how far it has gone, and what the probable outcome of it is to be, on the theory that the universe is sane.

Let us go back so many million years that

there is no use of even trying to count them
for the moment, to a time when the whole of
space that is now occupied by any part of the
universe that we can investigate with our
largest telescopes was fire-mist, chaos, containing neither planet nor sun, nor satellite of
any kind. The whole space filled with a mist
so heated that there were none of the minut-
est particles of it that were in contact with
each other, a gas so tenuous that it never
could be investigated. Then millions of years
roll away, the fire-mist moves and starts up
centres of rotation ; and by and by you have
somewhere in the midst of it a nebula, or neb-
ulæ, only a thicker condensation of fire-mist,
but with perhaps a centre a little more dense
than the outermost parts. The motion goes
on ; by and by the centre separates itself from
the outermost parts by its greater rapidity of
motion, and so flings off a ring,—such a ring
as you may discover around Saturn to-day.
This ring cools, breaks, its parts tumble together, and by their rotation assume the form
of a sphere and begin their motion around the
greater central mass. The central mass flings
off another ring, and that falls into fragments
and coheres into another sphere, and the central mass flings off another ring. This is the

process, they tell us, that had been going on in the formation of our little solar system, the outer ones flung off first and then another and another, until we got down to our little earth, which, in the process of its cooling, threw off a ring which condensed and made our moon.

Now, after thousands of years had gone by, this little earth of ours became cool enough so that certain kinds of life could live upon it in the ooze by the water's edge,—certain kinds of fish, tiny plants, tiny animals or animalculæ; and the process of cooling and of the evolution of life and its climbing from the lower forms to the higher went on. We have the fishes, the reptiles, and the birds, then mammals, all the gigantic animals, and then, at last, a feeble sort of being that did not know it was man, that we now call by that name,—feebler than almost all the other animals of its size. There had been a marvellous development of the brain; and, though it was weaker than almost all its enemies, it began to have the power to outwit its enemies, outknow, outthink them. Under the form of cunning it developed an ability to master the rest of the world. Then this cunning developed into the higher form, the intellect, which ruled mankind. Then this animal developed something higher than intellect,—

the power to love, and, out of love, came conscience; and this strange creature became a moral being. And then out of the moral being, and beyond it, began to appear a spiritual nature.

Remember, then, that there was a time when the mightiest power on the face of the earth was muscle; then there came a time when the mightiest power was a cunning that could outwit muscle; then a time of a higher form of intellect, which was superior to muscle or cunning; then love and a conscience, which was mightier than they, until to-day, in spite of all the evil that there is in the world, the mightiest power on the face of the earth is the moral ideal. The Czar of Russia, the Emperor of Germany, the Queen of England dare not go to war without appealing to the conscience of mankind, and claiming that the war is right and just. The moral ideal, then, in spite of what you may think this old world to be, is the mightiest power on the planet.

Now, the next step, the next logical, natural step, seems to me to be a development of the spiritual nature, provided man is a spiritual being, as I think we shall prove indubitably before we are through. If you had been present when cunning was beginning to outwit muscle, there was a long period of time when it would have been a question with you as to which would have come out ahead in this age-long battle. For you must not think these battles were decided in a year or a century. It was hundreds of thousands of years that this process was going on.

Suppose you had been present when one of these transition periods was passing by? What would you have found? You would have found here and there sporadic manifestations of the higher life, merely a promise, of the kind that makes you think of spring when you see the early buds. But there may come a storm, and all the blossoms be hidden after that. So you never would have been certain as to how long this process had been in taking place.

So we are to-day in regard to scientific study. The four thousand years of the world that we can clearly claim to be historical when compared with the time of the human race on this planet is not an hour in a day : it is rather one hour perhaps in a week. Is it not perfectly natural, then, that, beginning with the first we know of our human history, there should have been spasmodic, sporadic manifestations of what we call the spiritual nature of man, breaking through the guise of flesh ; that there should now and then, if we are whelmed and surrounded in a spirit world, appear a face, as in a glimpse, a voice be heard, a hand felt by someone more than usually psychically sensitive ? Is not this just what on that theory you would have expected ? Is not that the kind of progress of the world Paul outlines, when he says, " First the blade, and then the ear, and then " — long after that—" the full corn in the ear " ?

In other words, as an evolutionist, first, last, and all the time an evolutionist, I believe that we are to-day beginning to have manifestations of a new and higher, a more spiritual type of man that ought to be precisely what we should be looking for.   The world is getting ripe for it.   We are on the edge of it ; and I believe with my whole soul that it will not be long before immortality will be as much discovered as America was discovered by Columbus. These spasmodic manifestations that have been seen, and heard, and felt in all religions, in all races, for the last three or four thousand years, are just the first little blossoms of spring, frost-nipped, trodden under foot, and forgotten ; but they have been prophecy, and the prophecy of that which I believe is to come.

XII

THE SOCIETY FOR PSYCHICAL RESEARCH AND THE IMMORTAL LIFE

THE writer of the first Epistle to the churches of Thessalonica, in the fifth chapter and twenty-first verse, has used words which might well be the motto of this Society. They are words which are a justification for all scientific inquiry. They are words which are a condemnation of any blind faith or the acceptance of positions for which there is no evidence. These words are, " Prove all things." Prove all things: test all things, try all things, criticise all things, investigate all things. " Hold fast that which "—bears the test—" is good "; throw the rest away.

This has been the motto of science, of course, in all ages; but even to-day, so far from its being the motto of most religious thinkers, writers, speakers, it is the precise opposite. Recently, in one of the leading papers of the city, there was a discussion concerning the case of Dr. Briggs which took this ground : that a belief in immortality, the Bible as an inspired book, religious truth of any kind, simply could not be proved in accordance with the scientific method, or received on the basis of reason. And this was by a writer speaking in defence of the Church and of religion who said the Church, religion, the Bible, immortality,—all these things,—if received at all, must be received simply by faith,—that they cannot bear the test of reason. He would have gone on to say that they are above and beyond reason. After you have put reason out of court, what reason is there for believing anything, or believing one thing more than another? There is literally *no reason left*, after you have put it away. Therefore, literally, there is no reason why a man who takes this position should not accept Buddhism or Mohammedanism as well as Christianity. There is no reason left why he should believe anything,—no reason left why he should believe any one thing more than any other.

Therefore, the man who takes this position, it seems to me, goes a little too far for the defence of his own proposition. But this is the attitude that has been taken, not only toward most of the great religious problems of the world, by the Churches of the past and the great Churches of the present : it is the position that has been taken in regard to this very matter.

I received a private letter recently in which the writer said he had been corresponding with two of the great theologians of the country, one a Congregationalist, the other a Methodist, the Methodist being a bishop, and that both of them had said that they never expected to find anything like absolute proof of a future life,—they took it on faith, and did not believe that proof was possible.

So you see this same position of surrendering the possibility of proof extends, not only to most of the great Church dogmas, but to this question that agitates the hearts that have ever loved or ever lost, as to whether or no death is the end of all.

We have traced briefly, as has been necessary, in broad outline but with sufficient clearness, the beliefs of man from the beginning as to the life beyond death ; and we have come to this point, which is a most significant one. As I have already said, men have held all sorts of strange attitudes toward this profoundest of all questions. They have believed on what they called faith ; that is, the authority of somebody whose statements they have taken on trust. They have reverenced some of these claims as a part of their religion.   They have sneered at some as ghost stories, in the daylight and in companionship with their friends; they have cringed and cowered with fear lest such things as ghosts *might* be real, when they were alone and in the dark.   They have taken almost every conceivable kind of attitude toward these questions except one of rational inquiry.

It seems to me, indeed, most, striking that from the beginning of the world until within the last decade or two there has never been on the part of humanity anything like a serious investigation of a series of claimed facts, which, if true, or only partly true, are the most important facts in all the world.   Think of it! Until the year 1882, to be specific, whatever particular individuals may have done, humanity had never made a combined, serious, scientific attempt to find the truth in this great matter!

Some people have said that, if God had intended us to know, He would have told us about it in the first place.   Why not apply that to every problem?   God told primitive man very little.   He did not even tell him what was good to eat and what was poison : he had

to find it out by experience. He has absolutely, in this sense, told us nothing. He has
revealed Himself in the facts, the wonders, the
glorious on-going life of the universe, but has
left us to read these hieroglyphics, and find out
their meaning for ourselves. He has done
this in every department of thought and life.
Why not here?

Then there are a great many persons who
bravely tell us that, however interesting it is,
there is no use in trying to find out the truth in
any scientific way, because it is impossible of
discovery. How do they happen to know it is
impossible? Great men in the past have told
us that many things were impossible which are
every-day occurrences now. So we will not be
quite content to take it on the dictum of anybody that it is impossible to discover another
life.

If that other life be,—if it is not merely a
fancy or a dream,—why should we assume that
it is undiscoverable? I know no reason ; and
I believe that the human race will keep on in
its attempts, knocking at the door until it opens,
if any door there be. Humanity has been
advised ever since I can remember, and I presume for a good many centuries before that, to
give up trying to find the North Pole ; and it

has been said over and over again that it would
do no good to find it, anyway, and that it was
impossible to find it, even if it would. But
humanity has never given it up ; and it will not,
until it reaches there. So you may advise
humanity as much as you please to give up
seeking for an answer to this problem,—If a
man die, shall he live again ? I do not believe
it ever will be given up until the answer is
found.

It is a little curious that so many men, religious men, should tell us that it is impossible
—that they should believe a line in Shakespeare
rather than their own Bibles. I have heard it
quoted over and over again, as though it were
the summing up and the quintessence of all
wisdom, that it is "a country from whose
bourne no traveller returns." Yet this flatly
contradicts their Bibles and every religion on
the face of the earth ; for every one of them
assumes and teaches as facts that somebody at
some time has come from beyond that bourne
with a message to us here. And that is the
reason, deep down in their hearts,—literally,
the remnant of a tradition of that sort,—that
they believe. The only point is that they
assume that what God has done or what the
people have done over and over again cannot

be done now and is never going to be done
again.

With so much of preliminary, let me come
to indicate to you in outline, but with perhaps
sufficient clearness and force, so that you shall
see what it is about, the work of the Society
for Psychical Research.

This Society was organised in England in
the year 1882.   It was organised in this country
—and I was one of its corporate members,
having studied facts that it proposed to investigate for years before it was organised—in the
year 1885.

The first president of the Society in England
was Professor Henry Sidgwick, of Cambridge
University, and one of the greatest ethical
writers of this century.   Of the original vice-
presidents, five have died.   Among these was
Professor Balfour Stewart, one of the best
scientific men of his age ; another, Richard H.
Hutton, for many years editor of the London
Spectator, one of the great papers of England.
Two other original vice-presidents still occupy
their position,—the Right Hon. Arthur J. Balfour, one of the famous names in modern England, Member of Parliament, a Fellow of the
Royal Society ; and Professor W. F. Barrett,
of Dublin University.   Mr. Edmund Gurney,

who died in the midst of his work, and Mr. F. W. H. Myers are two other names famous around the world.   Mr. Myers I shall probably refer to again,—one of the great essayists and a well-known writer of the present time.

In this country we have not had so many great names : but we have accomplished some of the most important work right here among our-selves.   I will name a few : Professor S. P. Langley, of the Smithsonian Institution in Washington ; Professors Bowditch, Pickering, and Royce, connected with Harvard College ; and one of the keenest and most interested workers of all, perhaps the greatest psychologist living, the man who is recognised through-out Europe as well as America as a leader in that direction, and whose leadership is being recognised by the fact that he is to go to Ox-ford for the next two years and lecture there on his special theme,—Professor William James, a brother of the famous novelist, Henry James. Professor James H. Hyslop, of Columbia College, is another man engaged in this work.

There are also Lord Rayleigh, Professor Ramsey, F.R.S., and Professor Lodge,—one of the greatest mathematicians and physicists living in England at the present time.   One who has played an important part in the recent work of the Society over there, is Professor W. F. Barrett, of Dublin, who was active in starting the work both in England and here. One more I must speak of, because he is at present the president of the Society in England. This is Sir William Crookes, F.R.S., the inventor of the Crookes tube that has played so large a part in connection with the X-rays during the last two or three years, and who has occupied one of the foremost positions in the scientific life and work of England during the last twenty-five years.

In this country Bishop Brooks, Rev. R. Heber Newton, and others have been intensely interested in the work, and have added to it as much as they were able. And, while there are a great many people who for one reason or another think that this matter is hardly worth their time and attention, let me give you the word of a man like Gladstone,—Gladstone, the foremost statesman of his age ; Gladstone, who held in his hand problems of war and peace, not only in Europe, but in all the world ; Gladstone, the Churchman from head to foot, the orthodox believer in the Trinity, the Bible, Biblical and ecclesiastical tradition ; Gladstone, one of the greatest brains, one of the purest hearts, one of the keenest controversialists

of his time. He accepted an honorary membership in this Society,—honorary, because
he was too busy to do work connected with
it, but was glad to have his name associated
with it. And, in accepting it, he writes,
" It "—that is, the work of the Society for
Psychical Research—" is the most important
work which is being done in the world—by far
the most important." He, the stateman, watching the changes, the institutions, the growth,
the plots, the failures, the successes of nations ;
he, keenly interested in theological problems ;
he, looking at psychical research, and understanding all that science has accomplished,
with all its adventures and discoveries,—he
says that this one thing is the most important
work that is being done in the world.

I have told you that ; I have been saying it
for years ; but the opinion of a man like Gladstone carries weight with everybody who
thinks. Gladstone does not say, " I am a
Churchman, I have it in the Bible, I have it in
ecclesiastical tradition, and that is enough : "
but he says this work of yours done in attempting to prove it scientifically is the most important work in the world !

Now, what is the attitude of these men ?
Professor Sidgwick in his inaugural address,

challenged the world, saying to men of science
and men of thought everywhere :   Here are
certain strange alleged facts,—facts testified to
since the beginning of the world, facts testified
to in every nation to-day. Are they true ? Are
they false ? He challenged the scientific world
in England by the statement : It is a scandal
to intelligent, thinking men and students that
this problem should not be settled. It is a
scandal that the world should not find out
whether these things are true or not. And
this is the spirit in which he undertook the
investigation.

And remember that no member of this
society commits himself to a belief in anything.
He simply promises seriously and earnestly to
investigate with the one purpose, if possible,
of finding out what is true.   That is all.
That is the attitude which they took from the
beginning, and no member of the Society is
committed to the belief of any other member.
In other words, it occupies precisely the same
position that any great scientific organisation
occupies anywhere,—its one aim is truth.   It
is possible, for example, that an astronomer
may think he has made a discovery in the
heavens, and he reports this to the Society, but
the other astronomers doubt it.   They do not

think he has brought adequate proof yet ; and so they wait and study until the proof is overwhelming and all reasonable men are obliged to accept it, or until it is decided that it was a mistake in the first place, and that no sufficient evidence can be found. This is the attitude of this Society, then. So that, if towards the end I shall tell you the opinions of certain members of this Society, you will understand that they do not bind the opinions of anybody else at all, and that these men expect the world to be convinced only when sufficient evidence has been brought to bear down all unbelief and all opposition.

Now, what are the things that these men are studying? You know that not so long ago there was a man in France, by the name of Mesmer, who discovered what he called " Mesmerism," or what came to be called Mesmerism, after his name. It was scoffed at by all wise people as nonsense. A scientific committee of investigation was appointed ; and they looked the matter all through, as they supposed, and reported it all fraud and humbug. There is not an intelligent man on the face of the earth to-day, however, that does not know that it, and a good deal more, is true : only to-day it is called " hypnotism " instead of Mesmerism,"

—that is all ; and it is being used as a part of the medical armory, a storehouse of weapons against disease, by hundreds of the best physicians in France and Germany, in England and America.

Then there are many other facts. There are questions of the "subliminal consciousness," as it is called. We know that the mind works when we are asleep, or when our ordinary consciousness is engaged in attending to something else. So that this subliminal consciousness of ours became a fact for investigation. Then there are clairaudience, clairvoyance. There is the visible movement of physical bodies without any visible reason for their moving ; there is the playing of musical instruments by no visible fingers or hands ; there are visions, there are voices, there are scenes and experiences on death-beds ; there are what are called hauntings, wraiths, doubles, phantasms of the dead and of the living. There is no sort of question that there are phantasms of both the dead and the living ; but no scientific man takes that as proving immortality. It simply raises a question as to what they are and what they mean. But that what we call ghosts exist, no unprejudiced student has the slightest doubt.

So there are all these various fields of research.   There are the reports of houses that are haunted. There are trances, visions, voices, automatic writings.   These are claimed facts; and it is a little strange that they have been claimed from the beginning of human history, only they have never been seriously or scientifically investigated before.   I confess to you that it would be a relief to me to find out that there was truth in them, if only for the sake of finding out that the human race has not been crazy for ages.   If there is only a grain of truth, no matter how exaggerated the stories have been, it would run a luminant light of reason up along the path of the human race. Nobody doubts Tacitus, the Roman historian, when he talks of other things; and he tells these stories.   He was a little wild and credulous, as we say, when stories of *this* kind are told.   So we have been accustomed to throw them away instead of investigating and finding if there were not the shadow of some great truth in them.

Now, this Society for Psychical Research, both in England and America, set itself seriously about investigating these matters, just as they would investigate a bone of an animal dug up from the earth or the remains of a leaf preserved in a rock, or some other equally important matter. And I submit to you whether this matter is not as important as bones or petrified leaves or the dredging of the bottom of the sea, or any of the great objects of scientific research? But, when I find a man who devotes his life to the study of petrified leaves or the bones of animals, or to something of this sort, and who scouts and sneers at these great questions, it seems to me that he is exalting that which is little and belittling that which is great. For, if the Society for Psychical Research does no more, it has already unspeakably enlarged the boundaries of human thought concerning man himself. Up to the present time there has been no dark continent or "Darkest Africa" on the face of the earth so dark as the mind of man; and out of this mind of man have been coming reports and beliefs of ten thousand mysterious things, which have whispered and promised wonders beyond human imagination. Now, if we do nothing more than add new continents to our knowledge of human nature, it seems to me that is worth while. It seems to me that, only next to the question of immortal life, that is the most important subject on the face of the earth.

Now, I may put in a little of my own personal observation as I continue, although I am not to enter into personal detail concerning my own investigations here. Here are these claimed facts,—strange, indeed, if they are true, and strange, yes, perhaps stranger, in view of the fact that the world has always been accepting them, if they be *not* true. Now, how can we conceivably explain them? Take all these things that form the subject of the study of the Society for Psychical Research. How can these facts be explained?

First, you can explain them, as thousands of people do, by saying that they are all fraud from the beginning.

In the next place, you can explain a great many of them as being illusion, misconception on the part of the sitter or of the psychic.

Then, in the third place, you can range them under the theory of telepathy.

When you have passed telepathy, if you go beyond it at all, you are over the border-land in spite of yourself, and in the presence of invisible intelligences, all of whom always claim that they used to live here on this earth. Now, I know perfectly well, and the Society for Psychical Research has discovered over and over again, that there is any amount of fraud.

There are a great many people in this world
willing to get their living in what happens to
be the easiest way, and whether or no it neces-
sitates telling the truth or avoiding deception
of other people, does not seem to trouble their
consciences much. So, if there is an opportunity
to get an easy living by simulating or assuming
these things, you may be sure it is not lost.
The men who do business on Wall Street,
know that there are a good many such people
engaged in business.   Then, naturally, there
is a good deal of self-deception.   Unless a
person is experienced in the matter, when he
goes and sits with a psychic, he is pretty sure
to tell the psychic all that is necessary to be
known on the subject.   He "gives himself
away," as we say, by his tattle about himself.

Then there are a great many strange experiences which the psychic passes through for
which he or she flies off to the land of spirits
in search of an explanation, when an explanation could be found a good deal nearer home.
And you know it is one of the cardinal principles of science to seek the nearest, the easiest,
the most rational explanation.

But now we come to telepathy. I have
known intimately Dr. Richard Hodgson, who
is at the head of the Society in this country,

and who is one of the most careful scientific, sceptical investigators that I have ever known ; and he told me it was his avowed intention to explain every conceivable fact without having anything to do with spirits, if he possibly could. He was bound as a scientist to stretch every other theory until it broke before he would admit the possibility of our having to do with anybody who had passed beyond the border-land of what we call death. But the Society for Psychical Research has demonstrated over and over again that telepathy, at least, is true. I know it is true from my own experiences.

What does this mean ? It means that minds separate as far as from London to India communicate with each other, without even wireless telegraphy to help them ; that, in the case of sudden accident or death,—that is, when one soul cries out for its mate,—that mate hears and knows what is taking place. Now, if things like this happened only once or twice or thrice, or ten or twenty times, perhaps you would say it was mere coincidence ; but, when they happen a hundred or a thousand times, the coincidence theory grows more difficult than the other one.

And, in regard to the attempt of people generally to explain these super-normal facts,

I have found a great many explanations harder to accept than the original facts. I have felt about it somewhat as the old lady did who borrowed a copy of the *Pilgrim's Progress* with Scott's notes, which were intended to be explanatory and helpful. She brought the book back, saying she understood it all except the notes. I have the same feeling sometimes in studying these matters,—that they are plain enough except the explanations ; and they seem a good deal harder for me to accept than the natural, claimed fact.

I know a case of telepathy, I know it beyond question, between the Indian Ocean and this city of New York. We have not discovered the law yet. We have not brought it under control, any more than we have wireless telegraphy. I am not at all certain that we shall not by and by. Think what it means, you who are astonished at the telephone and telegraph and the thousand advances and discoveries of the world,—think what it means for two minds or two hearts or two souls to come into contact, when separated by the diameter of the globe. Is there any other wonder of the modern world to compare with it?

By way of suggestion as to a possible scientific explanation of it which may come by and by, let me say this. We know that when two musical instruments are placed a certain distance apart, and keyed so as precisely to correspond with each other, one will sometimes respond when the other is touched. It is possible that there may be such a thing as minds or brain molecules keyed to each other so that, when some great sorrow or anticipated evil or stress touches one of them, there is response in the other, no matter how great the distance that may separate them.

Telepathy, then, is established. Clairvoyance, clairaudience are established. Nobody who knows anything about them denies that they are true, whatever their explanation may be. There are people who see without eyes and hear without ears; that is, who see and hear apart from the ordinary use of the physical organs supposed to be necessary for the exercise of those functions. What does this mean? It just suggests, does it not, that, if the soul can begin right here to get along without the use of its ordinary senses, it may be possible for it to get along without them altogether? It suggests it, I say; it does not prove it. I think you must have heard the story of the Second Adventist who thought he would startle Emerson by telling him that the world was

coming to an end in a week or two. " Well,
suppose it is, my friend," was Emerson's reply.
" I think I can get along without it."

So it is possible, that if we can get along
without the use of the ordinary senses to a
certain degree, we might go farther, and say
that there is a way of living without these
bodies that so frequently seem to be the whole
of us.

But passing beyond telepathy, which the
Society for Psychical Research has proved beyond question, there are all the other subjects
for investigation — hauntings, ghosts, every
kind of vision and trance. If you will study,
you will find that an attempt has been made
to explain all these by telepathy. We have
come now to face the fact, however, that there
are many important things which certain people in the Society think cannot be explained
by telepathy. For instance, Frederick W. H.
Myers has published to all the world his belief
that, as the result of his investigations as a
member of the Society for Psychical Research,
there is no such thing as death. He thinks it
is scientifically demonstrated that those we
call dead are alive, and that occasionally, beyond any question, they communicate with us.
Professor Lodge, one of the leading physical

scientists and mathematicians of England, has come to the same conclusion. Dr. Hodgson, a graduate of Cambridge in England, who has travelled all over the world, and is one of the finest scientific investigators I have known, after fighting against this conviction for years, has at last published to the world that he is compelled by his facts to believe that those whom we call dead are alive; is compelled to believe that we do get communications from them now and then. He feels perfectly sure that he has had communication after communication with personal friends of his own, and that he has established beyond any scientific question the fact of personal identity.

Now, let me indicate to you a moment the direction in which this study leads. I investigated this matter years before there was any Psychical Society. I did it because my parishioners were coming to me for help and sympathy; and I found I ought to have something better than prejudice to give them. I never tried to get into communication with a personal friend, as dearly as I should love to do so. I have never made that my object. I have simply studied to find if there be any truth here.

Now, let me give you my word for one thing.

I have had psychics tell me so many times things which I knew there was no earthly possibility of the psychic's having ever known anything about, that it has become a commonplace to me: it does not astonish me any more than to talk through the telephone. It has happened hundreds of times, and I have pursued this question with the same rigid method by which I would study a brick or a bone: for I do not want to be fooled or be the means of fooling anyone else. So, up to this time, psychics have told me over and over and over again, and it has happened hundreds of times in the investigations of the Society, things which the psychic did not know, could not have known; but I have always said, when it happened to me: That is not enough. *I* knew it. And, possibly, though I do not know how, my mind may in some strange, mystic way have been reflected in the mind of the psychic —it may have been a case of telepathy or mind-reading. So I must have something more.

At last that which I sought for came. I have been told things over and over, perfectly natural things, things that concerned me and what claimed to be the teller on the other side. I have had important things told me that by

no possibility could the psychic—who was not
a public professional psychic at all, but a personal friend—have known, and which I could
not have known.   I have had, for example, a
thing like this told me : how a person was
feeling, and what a person was doing, two
hundred miles away at the time—a message
quicker than the telegraph could have brought,
that which by no possibility either of us could
have known.   I have had internal mental experiences of sorrow and trouble that were
buried in the heart of a friend, and of which I
had never dreamed, brought to me over and
over again.

Whether you have investigated it or not,
these things are facts ; and, if they are true,
they take us beyond mind-reading, they take
us beyond telepathy.   Think for a moment of
the kind of explanations I have had people
offer.   They have said, in the face of certain
facts I have given them, " How do you know
that your subliminal consciousness, that consciousness which is below what we ordinarily
call consciousness, your sub-conscious self—
how do you know that that sub-conscious self
does not tap Omniscience, and get at the facts
of the universe ? "   Such seem to me infinitely
more difficult explanations than the facts

themselves,—more strange, more *outré*, harder to accept or believe.

So, with me, it has come to this : that, after years of investigation, a large number of the leading thinkers, students, authors, scientists, physical scientists, chemists, mathematicians —great minds—have come to believe that there is no possible way of explaining that which has been over and over again proved to be fact, without supposing that they have been in communication with some invisible intelligence. That at present is my own belief. I do not hold it dogmatically. If somebody can give me an explanation for my facts, I will take it. I want only the truth. But I hold this at present as what a scientist would call a "provisional hypothesis," as an adequate explanation for my facts until I can get a simpler and better one. That they are *facts*, I know ; and that these facts take us over the border and whisper in our ears the certainty of immortal life, I believe. And I believe not on faith, not on the basis of tradition, not because of anything the Bible says ; though in saying this I am not criticising or depreciating the Bible. I believe because a fact has come to me and been handled by myself—a fact which I can explain in no other way.

If this be true, friends, as I have told you before, there are no other problems on the face of the earth that need trouble us. The moral problem as to whether God's government seems good and merciful or not is of no account in the face of the certainty of an immortal life and the chance of an immortal evolution; the question as to whether we are rich or poor is of no account; the question as to whether we are sick or well is of no account; the question of the loss of friends becomes diminished to a little temporary separation with the certainty of an everlasting union.

Believing this, death is wiped out; and an immortal career opens before us, leading to the highest heights that imagination can conceive, and suggesting that, when we have reached those, only something finer and better still remains.

XIII

POSSIBLE CONDITIONS OF ANOTHER LIFE

I TRUST that I shall be understood as not dogmatising, not assuming to tell you things which I claim surely to know. I speak with no authority. I give only what seem to me to be rational thoughts and theories concerning another life, of the fact of which I feel perfectly certain.

When we come to the last moment of life, as we call it here, I believe that we shall find it not a horror, not a pain, but only a lovely sleep. Those who have the best right to an opinion on this subject will always tell you that in ten thousand cases there is rarely any consciousness of suffering in the fact of dying. Let us, then, put away from us that one fear. We may suffer a good deal during the rest of our lives. I do not believe we shall suffer in the process of passing from this world to the next.

Neither do I believe that there is going to be any marked or sudden change in us. Were I to die at this moment, I believe that, on my first coming to consciousness in the other life, I should be simply just myself. I see nothing whatever in the fact or process of dying that should make any marked change in us, any more than, as I have said, our going to sleep last night and waking up this morning has made another kind of being of us.

I think we have distorted all our ideas of the other life by our theological speculations, and by supposing that death is a line, the moment we have crossed which, our destiny is fixed, and we are either devils or angels forever. I do not believe that we change. We carry with us our personal consciousness, our memory of what we have been, and who have been our friends, and those most closely associated with us. If I could be persuaded that I was to enter another life, and at the same time was to forget all about this one, and who I have been while here, I would not wish its possession. It would mean absolutely nothing to me. I believe that I shall wake up from that sleep conscious of the past, conscious that I am I, and remembering and loving those who were dear to me here.

Neither do I believe, as some seem to, that the going out into that other world is into a strange and lonely country. When we came into this world, we were expected. Our coming was prepared for, and we were welcomed into arms of love and tenderest care. I do not believe that the next step ahead in the universe is into something poorer than was the occasion of our coming here. So I believe that we shall find ourselves among friends, in a place that shall seem very much like home, with people who, as Robert Collyer has somewhere and at some time said, are " just folks like the rest of us," so that there will be no lonely or sad waking up for us when we reach that other country.

Now I wish to mark very distinctly one point that appears to me to be of great import-ance. We may be able, clearly, scientifically, beyond any question, to establish the fact of another life beyond this; and yet we may never be able to know very much about it in detail until we get there. I speak of this, and wish to speak of it with emphasis, because a thousand times the question is asked me, why, if anybody has ever reported from the other side, have they not told us all about it ?

Will you note carefully with me one fact ?

All our knowledge here is limited of necessity by our past experience, the experience of the race.   If I were to attempt to describe to you any new thing or any new place, I could do it only by comparing it with something with which you are already familiar ; and, just in so far as it was unlike anything with which you were familiar, just in so far it would be simply impossible for me to describe it to you so that you could have any intelligible idea of it.

Suppose, for example, that I should come back from a journey in Central Africa ; and should sit down with a friend, and say, " I found a very strange and curious thing there ; " and he should say, " Well, what shape was it ? " I would say : " It was not the shape of anything you ever saw.   It was a new shape."   " What colour was it ? " " It was a new colour." " What was it like ? "   " It was not like anything you ever saw."   Do you not see that it would be absolutely impossible for me to explain it to him, though I might know about it and might be absolutely certain of the fact ?

So, just in so far as this other life, which I believe is all around us, transcends the life with which we are familiar here, just in so far it is simply impossible for even an archangel to describe it to us, to give us an intelligible picture of it.

I sit down beside a Sioux Indian, and I talk to him about Herbert Spencer's philosophy. I may be familiar with it, but it is so far beyond any experience or development of thought that he has had, that it would be utterly impossible for us to understand each other. You sit down by a child of eight years, and let him ask you questions that imply twenty years of experience, and can you make yourself plain? *You* may know all about it. The child has had no experience in the light of which it could interpret the things that you would say. So it is nothing against the fact that some of us believe that another world has been discovered, and that occasionally a message comes from thence, that this message is not able to answer all the questions which curiosity may suggest.

In the nature of things, as I have said, it is impossible for us to understand or comprehend, or clearly picture to ourselves, anything whatsoever that transcends human experience. So you need not doubt the fact itself because you do not happen to know all about it and can find nobody who can tell you.

Where is this other country? The ancient

peoples, as we have seen, put it frequently below the surface of the earth, or away in some far space of the heaven, thinking that the rainbow might be a bridge over the abyss that led to this far-off paradise. Others have located it in Isles of the Blessed toward the sunset. In all conceivable places has the imagination of man located the other life. Our astronomy, an astronomy learned and demonstrated since the principal theological creeds of the time were formulated, has compelled us to change our conception as to the definite location of any possible or conceivable spirit world. I am inclined to believe that it is very near us. It may fold this old earth of ours round, as does the atmosphere. Not that the inhabitants of it are compelled to remain always in contact with the earth; for I believe that death releases us from the prisoning of one planet and makes us citizens of the universe. But I believe that this spirit world is all about us. It may be true, as Milton speculated when he said :

" Millions of spiritual creatures walk the earth
　Unseen, both when we wake and when we sleep."

Now, take a word of the most authoritative scientist of the age as touching this matter.

Professor Jevons is one of the greatest authorities of the world.   In his famous book called *Principles of Science* he says, "We cannot deny the strange suggestion of Young that there may be independent worlds, some possibly existing in different parts of space, but others perhaps pervading each other unseen and unknown in the same space."

Who is this Young that Jevons quotes? He is the man who controverted the theory of light which was held by Newton, and converted the world to his theory, which is the universally accepted one to-day.   In other words, he is one of the great names in the science of the world ; and he tells us that for anything our eyes and ears have to say to the contrary, we may be surrounded on every hand by other worlds, invisible, intangible to us.   We are so apt—we people who think we know—to be the fools of our senses.

Do you know that I can see, only after the ethereal vibrations reach a certain number in a second, and that the moment these vibrations pass beyond another certain number, I cease to see ? In other words, I can see a narrow space while these vibrations are kept within certain limits ; while on either hand the universe stretches off into infinity, invisible to our present sense. So I can hear within certain limits of ethereal vibrations ; up to a certain point I hear nothing. There is not produced on the drum of the ear the effect capable of being translated, —in the mysterious fashion of which we know nothing,—as *sound* to the brain. After a certain number of vibrations have been reached, all is again quiet to our senses. Huxley tells us that, if our ears were adapted to take in all the vibrations, the noises of the growing of flowers in the night would be as loud as a thunderstorm.

In other words,—and this is what I wish you to get from what I am saying,—there may be millions of spiritual creatures walking the earth, pervading the atmosphere all around us, real, thrilling and throbbing with life, a life more intense than any we know anything about or can dream of, and our present senses take no cognisance of them whatsoever. Do not imagine, then, that a person or a thing cannot exist, because you cannot see or hear or feel that person or thing.

Do these people inhabiting the other world have bodies ? I think so. I do not know what powers of imagination may be possessed by other people ; but what some people talk about as "pure spirit" means simply nothing at all

to me.   Is there anything unscientific or unreasonable in talking about the inhabitants of
this other world as embodied?   Nothing whatever, to a man who really understands what he
is talking about. Scientists are perfectly familiar with states of matter so ethereal that they
are not cognisant to any of our senses.   Thus
real though invisible bodies may exist. Ninety-
nine times in a hundred or nine hundred and
ninety-nine times in a thousand, perhaps, they
are humbug and fraud : but a " spirit " photograph is perfectly rational, and not in the
slightest degree unscientific.   I do not know
that there ever was a fact of that sort ; but it
is perfectly possible,—so far as science has
anything to say about it—for the sensitive
plate of a camera can see better than human
eyes. You can photograph an invisible star.
You can photograph the side of an old ship
after it has been painted over and over until no
human eye can detect the lettering underneath ; and the photograph will show that
which is covered by the coats of paint. A
camera, then, may see better than we can.

Let me give you one instance in this direction as a suggestion. Alfred Russel Wallace is
the most famous scientific man living on earth
to-day. He made independently, and at about

the same time, the discovery that Darwin made ; and from the Isles of the Southern Sea he sent home to Darwin a paper to be read at the British Association, setting forth this discovery. At this same time Darwin was writing his book, not knowing that anyone else was thinking the same thoughts. So this man shares, and will always share with Darwin the glory of discovering the central principle of evolution. He told me in conversation some years ago that he had carried on this practice of attempting to get photographs of the other world, with a friend in a private house, month after month ; and he said, " I got a perfectly recognisable photograph of my own mother, which was utterly unlike any picture taken of her during her life." If true, this could not have been a copy of anything in existence—except his mother. This is Wallace's testimony, which you may consider for what it is worth.

So it is perfectly possible, I believe, that the inhabitants of the other world are embodied in some ethereal way, which we, perhaps, cannot understand to-day, and that they thrill and throb with life, in comparison to which this life of ours may seem to them almost a sleep.

Now comes another question. I have been

asked it thousands of times I suppose. If our
friends are about us and can see our suffering
and struggle and temptation and disappoint-
ment and tears, how can heaven be heaven to
them? Before answering that question, as I
intend to do, let me ask another. Which
would you rather do, if you could have your
choice when you leave this world—go away
somewhere so far off that you can not by any
possibility know what is happening to your
loved ones, or would you rather be near by,
even though they were suffering and you
shared in part their pain? I would rather be
where I could know what was happening to
my wife and children and friends, even if they
were in trouble, than to be away off in some
delectable spot in space, trying to forget about
my loved ones here, in order that I might be
happy. That would be no heaven to me.

But here is another answer which seems to
me absolutely conclusive. A mother, as she
sits in her home with her little child playing
at her feet, sometimes has an experience like
this. The child breaks her doll or plaything
of one kind or another; and this is a heart-
breaking sorrow to the little one; but it does
not break the heart of the mother at all. She
picks the child up in her lap, clasps her to her

heart, soothes and comforts her. She knows that it is but a passing sorrow, and is not going to cloud the child's life forever. So it seems to me that those who have found out to a certainty what the grand issue of life means, cannot be troubled because we shed a few tears over a loss in Wall Street or because we have a pain which may last us for a week. They know what is before us, they know it is to be victory in time ; and perhaps they know that these experiences of suffering that we are passing through, are part of the training that is to make us capable of entering into the joy and felicity which they have found their own.

There is another question. People ask me again and again—and I am answering these questions as though I believed—if the people in the other world, my friends in the other world, can communicate with anybody, why don't they come directly to me ? Why must they go to a psychic, a stranger, somebody about whom I know nothing ?

In the first place, I tell you frankly, I do not know anything about it. But I have a theory which seems a me a very reasonable one. Let me ask a counter-question. If electricity will run along a wire—I am using the old theory that electricity is a fluid, but I do not know what it is and do not know of anyone who does—if electricity can convey a message from Chicago to New York over a wire, why cannot it convey it over a board fence? I do not know; and there is nobody in the world who does know. We simply know the fact, and, knowing that, we do not waste our time trying to operate over board fences. If we want a message from a friend in Chicago, we expect it to come over the wire.

Now, why cannot my friend come directly to me? I do not know; but, supposing the fact, my theory of it is this. I believe that what we call psychic sensitiveness — that is, the ability to be impressed in a conscious way— might be compared to musical sensitiveness. Almost all persons have a little sense of musical sounds; but there are very few who can master instruments or who can sing so that anybody wants to hear them—very few, indeed. But will you go without music because you must go to the experts, the masters, the musical geniuses, to get it? Or will you sit at home, and say, "I will not have any music until my next-door neighbour can furnish it or I can furnish it myself?"

I do not know why we know only certain

facts. I believe that this psychic sensitiveness is something that we all share within certain limits, but that there is only occasionally psychic genius, one so sensitive that he or she is usable, so to speak, in a practical way. That is my theory of it. I do not know why, but I do know the fact; and I have known people—and I must indicate the unreasonableness of it in passing —I have known people who said, " A friend of mine died ten years ago, and promised that, if it were possible, he would communicate with me, and let me know that he was really alive ; and I have heard nothing from him." And I have said over and over again, " Have you ever given him a chance ? and, if you have not, what right have you to find fault that he has not reported ? Perhaps it is your fault, and not your friend's."

There is another point here. I believe that these friends of ours are ministering spirits. Not that they stay always by our side, but that many of them may be ministering spirits watching around us, rendering us service of which we have little knowledge, which we cannot comprehend or explain to-day. They may interfere sometimes to render us a signal service. To illustrate what I mean, and to show what seems to me to be a more rational

theory than that commonly held—some people believe that there have been "provid-
ential" interferences in their lives — certain
things have happened which seemed inexplicable to them, at any rate ; and they wonder
whether God has been caring for them in
some special way. Now, I cannot think of
God as partial.   I cannot think that He hears
the prayer of one person, and turns a deaf ear
to the heart-breaking cry of thousands.   That
does not seem to me worthy of our thought
about God.   And yet there do happen these
strange coincidences.   I have a friend, Mrs.
Mary A. Livermore, famous for her devoted
services during the war, and one of the greatest woman speakers that the world has ever
known.   She told me how her life was saved
during her travels in the West on a certain occasion by her hearing and instantly
obeying a voice.   She did not know where it
came from ; but she leaped, as the voice or-
dered her to, from one side of a car to the
other, and instantly the side where she had
been sitting was crushed in and utterly demolished.   This she told me.   I cannot believe
that this was the interference of God ; but it
may have been the interference of some friend
in the invisible.   And this may account for

the fact that interferences happen at some times, and not at others.

Suppose I am on the street to-morrow, and an accident happens to me. A friend may be in the neighbourhood, and see it and come to my rescue. But the friend may *not* be there. There may be no one cognisant of the fact, so no rescue may come to me. This seems to me a possible and very rational theory of accounting for what we call special providences or interferences on our behalf.

And there may be a grain of truth in the Catholic doctrine of the saints. If I cry for help in my need, and a friend knows that I cry, and recognises that need, and can help me, and does help me, my prayer is answered; though it may not have been by the interference of God in the ordinary sense of that expression. So, possibly, these heart-cries of ours, that go up into what to us is the silence, may reach the ears and touch the hearts of the friends who are not so far away as we ordinarily imagine; and out of that unseen there may frequently come to us help and comfort and strength.

These are possibilities. I have not said one word thus far that any scientific man on the face of the earth has any right to contradict.

He may tell me, and tell me truly, that I have said a good many things that I cannot demonstrate; and I grant it. But he cannot demonstrate that they are *not* true. He cannot prove the negative; and he cannot prove them to be unreasonable. They are perfectly within the possibilities of the universe as we know it scientifically.

Now, let us raise the question as to what it means to go over and live in that other life. Most of us, I suppose, have given up all fear of the old orthodox place of fire and torment; but we carry in ourselves heavens and hells, and, though we may put out the fires of the infernal regions, we do not thus put out the fires in our own bosoms which we ourselves have kindled. So, if we wish happiness in that other life, we must cultivate that in us which is spiritual and which is good. It is sometimes said that much of the life we lead here will be of no use to us over yonder. It has been said, concerning certain men, "They made themselves wonderful scholars in certain directions; but they died young, and now what is the use of it all?" As though any experience could be thrown away! I do not believe it is thrown away at all. A man may cultivate himself by following some certain line. If he cultivate himself nobly and rightly, that general development of power may be just as valuable to him in some other pursuit, or in some other condition of life, as it is here.   So that all the intelligence that we have wrought out, all the development of self-control, of character, of nobility, of love, of goodness—these things are imperishable, and are, perhaps, those which Jesus had in mind when he advised us to lay up treasures in heaven, and not on the earth —to lay up the treasures that are invisible in the place that is at present invisible, and where we may take them up and find them of value on our arrival.

In that famous thirteenth chapter of First Corinthians, Paul says, " If we have knowledge, it shall pass away." He is discussing things that pass away and those that remain.   He is right in certain directions. I may develop all kinds of knowledge in this life, and in the other land I may find myself in circumstances where that knowledge is of no value at all ; but the *cultivation* I have gone through in acquiring that knowledge may be of unspeakable value to me.

The intelligence, then, we may believe we carry with us. But, says some objector,—it is said a thousand times, printed in review articles, spoken of in lectures,—" How can we think without the brain?   Is not the brain the only organ of thought?"   Professor James, of Harvard, whom I have often quoted, has a lecture on two phases of this problem of the other life; and one of them is this phase: and he—one of the best expert authorities in the world—takes the ground that the objection about the brain is foolish, sophistical, shallow, and utterly worthless.   In other words, *one* of the functions of brain at the present time may be thinking.   The " I " that is back of the brain, or above it, may use it as the organ of thought and the communication of my thoughts to others in my present condition.   But that does not prove at all that the " I " ceases to exist, and that there is no thinking done, when this brain gets tired and goes back to dust. To resort to a crude illustration,—you may attach a dynamo for a time to some particular machine.   When you have removed that machine, you have not destroyed the dynamo. You may attach it to some other machine, and find that you have there all the old-time power.

The best scientific men of the world have told us that this objection is of no value. Thought is not the product of the brain, in that sense.   There accompanies every effort of mind certain molecular movements in the brain. That is all. But it is not a case of cause and effect; it is only concomitance. Thought coincides with the movements of the brain.

We may carry, then, with us, all our magnificently developed powers of thought. We carry love, which is the grandest thing in all the world and is the heart of heaven, whether that heaven be here or somewhere else. We carry with us pity and tenderness and sympathy. We carry all those things that we call spiritual, that are of value to us, that constitute our nobler and higher selves. The rest we leave behind, because we have got through with it, and do not need it any more.

A word must be said as to possible occupations in the life beyond death. The Swedenborgians, following the great seer, tell us that heaven is almost a duplicate of the present life; that almost all the occupations that we carry on here are carried on in some fashion over there.

I believe that the thinker carries with him his great power to think, and that there will be opportunity for ranges of thought there that so surpass all that is conceivable to us to-day as to seem to us almost incredible. The thinker may study, investigate, and discover the natural laws of the universe under conditions of which we can hardly dream to-day.

I will give just a natural hint. Old ex-President Hill, of Harvard, was one of the most famous mathematicians of the century. I am afraid I should not enjoy his company, nor he mine, should I find him engaged in his favourite occupation on the other side. But this is what he said. Somebody asked him, " What are you going to do when you enter the other life ?" And his reply was, " There are enough problems, mathematical problems, connected with the arc of a circle, to keep me busy and happy for at least a thousand years."

That was one of the most famous mathematicians of the century. Why should the musician lose the enjoyment of his transcendent power? Why the artist of his? Why should any of the magnificent souls of the world find themselves without occupation ?

And then, I believe another thing. There are sainted souls, men and women both, in this life, who would not find themselves happy if there were not somebody to help, somebody to whom they could be of service. This condition of mind is illustrated, although humorously, in the expression of the old sainted Calvinist deacon, who had made up his mind that he had committed the unpardonable sin, and was sure that he should go to hell. Some one asked him what he should do there, and he said he should try to start a prayer-meeting. The dominant wish and will of the soul, I believe, will find scope for its inclination.

Remember how many millions of little children are passing into this country every year. They would need nursing and care and teaching if they stayed here. I believe they will need, and will find, nursing and teaching and care and tenderest love over there. And there are thousands of men and women dying uneducated, undeveloped, soiled, and vicious. Perhaps it is not their own fault. They may have inherited weakness, and been brought up in surroundings that made virtue practically impossible. I believe there will be opportunities for ministering to such as these.

Then, sometimes, when we get very tired, we think that we would like a long time, at least before doing anything again, for rest. As an illustration of this state of mind, I received a letter from Edward Everett Hale during the winter of 1899, in which he said: "When we get to heaven and have been there a few æons, and had a chance to get rested a little and to look around us, I hope I shall have an opportunity to get off with you in some secluded place and have a leisurely talk about some things that I despair of ever getting hold of here."

So this leisurely rest, this thrilling, throbbing occupation of love and service, this thirst of the discoverer, of the inventor, this genius of the artist, the musician,—all that is noblest and finest and sweetest here, I believe it is not at all unreasonable for us to suppose will find ample scope and unfolding over yonder. Much of it, most of it, of course, is guess-work now.

We are surrounded with mystery on every hand; and sometimes we get discouraged because we cannot answer all our questionings. Get discouraged! Think of it, think a little further, think a little deeper ; and this, which is your overwhelming difficulty. at times, you will see to be the source and spring of every rational hope. Suppose that we could get through over there in a year or a thousand years ; suppose there were no more questions to be asked, nothing more to be done, nowhere else to go. We should pray for a death that would stay death, from sheer *ennui*.

The only rational ground for belief in the possibility of an immortal life is in the fact that we are surrounded on every hand by alluring mystery, and a mystery that in certain senses may grow and increase as the ages go by. I am in a little valley. I cannot explain how the grass grows or the flowers bud and spring. I could ask a thousand questions that I could not answer; but my difficulty seems to me little and somewhat comprehensible. I climb up the mountains; and the range in the mystery of the unknown grows with every step of ascent.

So I believe that, as we advance, the mystery of the universe, and of our tender, loving Father, God, will increase, instead of diminishing at every step. So I can believe that the hope of an immortal life is a sensible hope, because I know that I can study and think and advance forever and ever and ever, and never approach getting through; for there is no possibility of "getting through" with the Infinite.

So let us be content with so much as must be mystery, not be discouraged by it,—but regard it as what it is: the ground of our noblest and most magnificent hope.

APPENDIX

SOME HINTS AS TO PERSONAL EXPERI-ENCES AND OPINIONS

I WAS a boy in the town of Norridgewock, on the Kennebec, in Maine, when I first heard of what has come to be called Spiritualism. My curiosity was aroused, but not in any serious way. I saw table-tipping, and heard raps, and knew that there were some people in the village who believed that they were by these means in communication with the spiritual world. I saw enough at that time to know that some force was in action other than that which we ordinarily call muscular power, whether conscious or unconscious. A small table which we had in the house would move, and answer questions in various ways, for myself. I have never been able to explain what then occurred by any ordinary means. I remember that on one occasion I stood up and touched a table very lightly with the tips of my fingers, and that it followed me quite across the room.   So much for my first knowledge of anything of this sort.   Of course, I do not offer this as scientific evidence of anything.

I had nothing more to do with the matter for a good many years.   Indeed, all my religious training gave me a decided prejudice against it.   And when I was a young minister in California, I demolished the whole matter, to my own satisfaction and to the satisfaction of a large number of enthusiastic hearers—the only "out" about the affair being that the hearers and myself were entirely ignorant of the whole subject.   We were correspondingly confident, however, as I have a good many times in my life found that ignorant persons are.

It was not, then, until 1874 that my attention was called to the subject again.   I had just moved from Chicago to take the ministry of the Church of the Unity in Boston.   One of my parishioners had lost her father.   She came to me one day and said that she had been visiting a certain "medium," whose name she gave me, and that some things had been said which seemed to her very remarkable.   She asked my advice, wishing to know whether I thought she had better pursue the matter further, or if I was acquainted with any reasons sufficient to induce her to drop the matter, as questionable or dangerous. I suddenly awoke to the consciousness that I had nothing better to give her than a prejudice. She asked for advice, and I was not competent to help her. I said frankly, " I do not know anything about it. I have always been prejudiced against it, I have preached against it ; but I have no knowledge on the subject whatever." And it then occurred to me that, as a minister of a congregation, I might be expected to be able to give advice on so important a subject.

I reflected that there were thousands—the claim reached even to millions—of persons in the modern world who were either believers in or were investigating the subject. I reflected also that it was either the grandest truth or the most lamentable delusion of the world which was involved. I made up my mind that I would take steps to have an opinion on the subject which was worth something, being based at least on somewhat of study and experience. Thus I might be able to guide the members of my congregation who came to me for advice.

This was twenty-five years ago. Since that time I have been a careful and close student of the whole range of psychical phenomena, so far as time and opportunity have permitted. I have not felt at liberty to neglect my regular work for the sake of it ; but I have felt that it was an important part of my regular work to know something of such matters as these. I came to feel that these problems were worthy of the most serious study, whether they took us across the border-line and gave us any knowledge of the other life, or stopped short and concerned themselves only with the powers of the mind as embodied. In either case they seemed to me remarkable. The darkest of all Dark Africas is the brain, and the mind whose activities are so intimately connected with it. So I never could quite understand why scientific men should slight or treat with contempt such remarkable facts as I knew existed, even though the spiritualistic claim might prove to be entirely unfounded.

I will now give an account of certain facts with which I have become familiar in the range of my own personal experience, following in some general way what appears to be the order of their importance. I am not so sure of the rank which they ought to hold, however, as some persons appear to be. But that does not matter.

In the first place, then, I will note certain things which come under the head of physical phenomena. I have already touched on the matter of table-tipping, raps, and matters of that sort. My experiments in this direction have been many, and have been scattered over a good many years. I know, beyond any question or qualification of the statement, that physical objects have been moved in such a way as was inexplicable on the theory that only the muscular power of any person present was involved. And here let me make a statement which seems to me of the utmost importance. *If so much as a hair or a grain of sand be moved, though it be only a fraction of an inch, by any power which is not "physical," in the scientific sense, then it seems to me that we have crossed the Rubicon that separates our ordinary life from what is called the "spiritual."* And if this movement be under the guidance of intelligence, then it demands something more than physics to account for it.

I have known of a party of people sitting around a table in frolicsome mood, until the table at last seemed animated by a force which they could neither guide nor control. I have known these same people to flee from the room at last in terror, shutting the door behind them, while objects in different parts of the house, upstairs and down, were flung about by some force that none of the people present could see or comprehend. Phenomena like these are credibly reported as having taken place in the house of old Dr. Phelps, the father of Professor Phelps of Andover, and in the home of the Wesleys in England.

A very prominent Liberal preacher of this country, whose name would at once be recognised as familiar to everybody if I felt at liberty to mention it, once told me that in the city of New York, in brilliant light, he and five or six other men sat on the top of a square piano which, with its human burden, was lifted into the air when a frail and delicate lady simply touched it with her fingers. This he testified to as a fact in his own experience, while at the same time he lived and died without any belief in a spiritualistic explanation of the fact. I refer to it simply as giving the testimony of somebody beside myself to such occurrences as these, whatever the explanation of them may be.

Another gentleman of my acquaintance, a scholar, a man of wealth, who had travelled and had lived much abroad, looked with contempt upon all these matters until they were

forced upon his attention through the " medi-
umship " of his own son, a lad of thirteen or
fourteen at the time. This man weighed at
least two hundred pounds, and he told me
that a large study table, which he pointed out
to me,—a very heavy table, containing drawers,
—had been lifted into the air and moved in
various ways around the room, with him sitting
on it, while his son merely touched it with the
tips of his fingers.

I myself, sitting in a heavy stuffed arm-
chair, in broad daylight, have been lifted
several inches from the floor, and set down
again as gently as though Hercules were
engaged in the process, the only visible reason
for it being that the " medium," sitting beside
me, laid his hand gently on the back of the
chair. This was done while a friend was
sitting by and keeping a keen watch. I have
on one occasion seen a chair lifted six inches
or a foot from the floor and brought across
the room, at my own request, and leaned up
within an inch or two of my side against the
table, in the position of a chair that is reserved
for some guest at the table of a hotel ; and
this without anyone's being within a great
many feet of it, and in broad daylight.

One more instance in this direction ; but

let me say that it seems to me hardly fair to
speak of these as purely physical phenomena,
because the movements indicate purpose and intelligent guidance, whatever may be the cause.
An English gentleman once told me that
he had seen an accordion played upon when
no hand was touching the keys. At the time
I did not believe a word of this. I did not doubt
the honesty or the intelligence of the gentleman
who told me; the matter simply appeared to
me incredible, and I thought that there must
be some mistake. Afterwards, however, I
became familiar with the published reports of
experiments carried on with Home, by Professor (now Sir William) Crookes, one of the
most famous scientists and chemists in the
world. His name has become recently familiar
to us, through the use of the Crookes tube,
his invention, in connection with the Roentgen
rays. Professor Crookes arranged scientific
apparatus by which to test the question as to
whether there was any force at work in the
presence of Home other than conscious or unconscious muscular power. He proved, beyond
question, that there was.

Among the experiments which he tried was
the one to which I have referred above, of the
playing on an accordion. He testifies that the

accordion was placed in a wicker basket (perhaps a common scrap-basket) under the table, and beyond the reach of anyone, and that while so placed tunes were played upon it without any visible touch. At last I had an experience of my own, which demonstrated that this was not only possible, but true. I was sitting with a "medium" one morning about ten o'clock, while the sun streamed into the room through large and numerous windows, so that there was no darkness or concealment. An accordion lay on the table. I took it up, slid the movable side out, held it up to the light, and examined it in every particular, to see that it was a simple, plain accordion. Then the "medium" took it in one hand, holding it by the side opposite to that on which the keys were arranged, and while it was within three or four feet of my face and in plain view, it played tune after tune, the accordion being pulled out and pushed in as though held by a hand on the other side. I then said, "Won't they play for *me?*"—assuming the existence of invisible intelligences who had been producing the music. His answer was, "I don't know; you can try if you wish." Thereupon I took the accordion and held it as he had done. No tune was played; but I had an experience which was even more conclusive as to the existence of some force which I could not comprehend than as if I had heard the music repeated.   Something, some power, or somebody—I leave it to the reader to decide—seized the accordion, and I found myself engaged in a struggle which required all the muscular power I possessed to enable me to keep possession of the instrument without its being torn to pieces.   It was as real a struggle as though a visible man had been attempting to take it away from me.   I do not assume to say what was at work while I held the accordion ; but I raise the question as to whether anything besides intelligence plays tunes.

Perhaps these are sufficient as specimens of what are ordinarily called physical phenomena. I could give dozens of others, but it is not necessary.

The time will doubtless come when this class of facts will be tested by a series of scientific experiments and their value be determined.   Meantime I mention this only as part of my story.

Now I wish to say a word or two in regard to the matter of raps.   And let me say here, in general, that I may repeat certain things that I have spoken of in my little book called

Psychics, Facts, and Theories, or that I have mentioned in the course of some of the chapters in this present book. Sometimes repetition plays the needed part of emphasis.

I was once passing through the city of New York (this was a good many years ago), when I called, one morning, with a note of introduction, on a lady who was widely known as a psychic. We were utter strangers to each other, except for the brief note of introduction which I had presented. She invited me into the back parlour, which was separated from the front by sliding doors. As we sat and conversed, I began to hear raps in various parts of the room. As some carpenters were at work on the conservatory, which was an extension of the back parlour, making more or less noise, she suggested that we adjourn to the front parlour, which would be a little more quiet. This we did, she sitting down in a rocking-chair, while I sat in another, some ten feet away. The raps again began ;—so far as my senses reported, they were on the floor, on the table, on the walls in different parts of the room. Some wise men have said (I have recently read it again in a newspaper) that these raps were produced by some unusual manipulation of the toe-joints. I do not care to take the trouble to deny this; but I would like to raise the question as to how it happened that her toe-joints were able to tell me a large number of things that the owner of the said joints could never by any possibility have known. For, in answer to my questions, the raps did answer questions and tell things which indeed I knew, but which I am perfectly certain that she did not know.

This has been the trouble always, to my mind, in explaining the matter of these raps. That they exist, everybody who has cared to investigate the matter knows. And I know, if everybody else who has written on the subject does not, that they indicate and express intelligence. Whether it is the intelligence of the sitters, or of some spirit power in another world, I am not prepared now to decide.

I will pass now to certain things which are generally regarded as belonging to a higher grade of these phenomena. It is thought by many that hypnotism is in some way connected with these experiences, so I may give it a passing word. When Mesmer first created a popular excitement in France, a great scientific commission was appointed to investigate the matter. It was done, to the satisfaction of the commission; and the decision was reached that the whole thing was fraud or illusion. To-day there is not a sensible scientific man in the world who does not know that even more wonderful things than Mesmer discovered are true, while doctors are using this mysterious power in the treatment and cure of disease. I have known cases where a person in the hypnotic condition was clairvoyant, though he did not possess the power in his ordinary state. This would seem to indicate that there may be some connection between these different forms of sensitiveness.

Clairvoyance and clairaudience exist, beyond question. I do not mean by this to endorse all the people who advertise themselves as possessing these powers and as undertaking to find lost objects or to give business advice to the credulous. I simply mean to state that there are such powers. Of course, I do not claim that they necessarily take us across the border-line of the present life.

The next point that this brings us to deal with is what is called telepathy or mind-reading. I believe that the experiments of the Society for Psychical Research have established, beyond any reasonable doubt, the fact that a power like this does exist. I have known cases, within the range of my own personal experience, and I have learned that distance has very little to do with them. Such mental communication can take place between England and India, between the Indian Ocean and the city of New York, or between widely separated States in our own country. I make these special allusions as indicating cases with which I am familiar.

I have myself been inclined to believe that these may be explained by physical means—that is, apart from the thought side, which I do not regard as physical. The communication may be by means of wave motions in the ether between brains which are, so to speak, attuned to each other, just as it is known that musical instruments will sometimes respond when they are pitched to the same key. I do not dogmatise in this matter : it is enough for my purpose simply to call attention to the fact that such things do exist.

Next, I will barely suggest the subject of ghosts or apparitions. I think there is no sort of question that there are such things as ghosts. What they are, or how they are produced—whether they are the real appearances of persons who have become inhabitants of what we are accustomed to call the spirit world, I do not always feel sure. A telepathic origin for some of them has been suggested, and in some cases perhaps with reason. But I have known cases where a friend, who was living at a distance, has appeared very soon after the fact of death, to someone in another town or another State. I have myself personally investigated and satisfied myself of the truth of happenings of this sort.

In this connection it may be worth while to speak of the visions of the dying. It is well known, of course, that persons suffering from fever and different kinds of illness have visions which are probably caused by the disease, and so are purely subjective. It is held by many that all visions of the dying are of this order. Dr. Clarke, a famous Boston physician, published some years ago a small volume entitled *Vision*. It contained an introduction by Oliver Wendell Holmes. Both Dr. Clarke and Dr. Holmes were inclined to think that the ordinary visions of the dying are of the subjective sort ; but both of them intimated that they had known certain cases where there was at least room for serious doubt as to whether the eyes of the dying were not looking upon some objective fact.

A good many cases have come under my personal observation. Most of them were not of a nature to prove that the dying person actually saw the friends whose names he called, or whose faces and forms seemed to him to be present. But I have known one or two cases that seemed to me to possess very remarkable features in the direction of proof. I will simply give one of them as a specimen.

There were two little girls, about eight or nine years of age, who lived in a city of Massachusetts. They were not relatives, but were very close personal friends. Both were taken ill at the same time with diphtheria. One, whose name I will speak of as Jennie, died on Wednesday. The family, the nurses, and the physicians all took special pains to keep the fact from her playmate, fearing that the effect of it might stand in the way of her recovery. It proved that they were successful in their efforts; for on Saturday morning, not long before the death of the other child, she went through the form of making her little will. She spoke of certain things that she wished to give to different ones among her brothers and sisters and playmates. Among these she pointed out certain things of which she was very fond, that were to go to Jennie—thus settling all possible question as to whether or no she had found out that Jennie was not still living.

A little later she seemed to be between the two worlds, seeing the friends that were about the bed, and also seeing those who are ordinarily invisible. She spoke of her grandfather and grandmother, and of others, expressing her delight to see them. And then she turned to her father, with face and voice both expressing the greatest surprise, and exclaimed, "Why, Papa, why did n't you tell me that Jennie had gone? Jennie is here with the rest! Why did n't you tell me of it?" This seems to be a case a little out of the ordinary. If she had known that her friend was among the dead, we might say with some reason that she was merely imagining that she saw her face among others that she believed had long been inhabitants of the other world. But her surprise at seeing this particular face carries with it the suggestion of reality, such as does not attach itself to the ordinary cases.

I know also of a case of a little boy, but two or three years old, who had been put to bed and was asleep. He had a friend, a Judge of some prominence, living in the place, who, having no children of his own, was very fond of this particular little boy,—used to come often to see him, bring him presents, and make a pet of him. On this evening the father and mother were sitting in the next room, when they heard the little boy crying violently, as though suddenly aroused from his sleep. They went in and found him sobbing as though his heart would break. They asked him what the matter was, and he called out, " Judge—— says he's dead! He has been here and told me that he is dead!" The next morning it was found that the Judge had died at about that time the night before.

It is worthy of note that these cases seem to have an evidential quality when connected with little children that they do not possess in the cases of grown people. The grown folks, it is presumed, have thought of these matters, as children have not, and have come to possess certain theories, ideas, and prepossessions in regard to them, which might produce or determine the nature of the visions.

I come now to consider such cases as Spiritualists are accustomed to consider communication direct from the other life. I have said and published a number of times that I am not a Spiritualist. I will take the trouble of saying it, and emphasising the matter, once more, because in spite of my previous assertions I find myself constantly represented by the daily papers as being one. Indeed, one of the papers, last winter, curiously enough, had it in big headlines that I was a thorough believer, while ten lines below, in the report of what I had said, was the explicit statement that I was not. While the newspapers herald their news in this fashion, it is no wonder that people occasionally get misrepresented. I say I am not a Spiritualist, not because I am afraid of any name, or would shun any stigma that might attach to a particular association ; but the word "Spiritualist," as ordinarily used, covers so many things which I do not believe, so many methods with which I am not only not in sympathy but to which I am strongly opposed, carries with its popular significance so much unreasoning credulity, the general movement so opposes itself to any scientific investigation, has covered and defended so many proven frauds, that I should misrepresent my position if I were willing to be known by the name. At the same time I am perfectly willing to say that I believe that there is a great truth at the heart of the Spiritualistic movement. And among the worst enemies of this truth, among those who stand most in the way of its rational acceptance by sensible people, are certain classes of Spiritualists themselves.

I must not go into this matter too much in

detail. I have received through psychics, over and over and over again, communications which I know, beyond question, did not come from the minds of the psychics themselves. That is, they were things with which, in the nature of the case, they could not possibly have been familiar. I do not deny that some of these may reasonably be credited to mind-reading or telepathy. In some way, although I know not how, they may have gotten hold of these facts hidden in the recesses of my own mind. It is a little curious to me, however, to note how glibly people will fly to mind-reading or telepathy to explain facts for which they are not willing to concede an explanation which assumes communication from the other side. And yet telepathy is as mysterious as the other theory, and as little known.

And let me say right here that it has always seemed to me a little strange to see people fighting so hard against accepting any evidence of the existence of their friends in another life, while at the same time they claim to believe that they do exist. I have had, as I said, hundreds of communications, stating facts which the psychic could not possibly have known. I have always said in regard to these that while immensely interesting, and while they might possibly come from beyond the border, they were not that which I was seeking—cases which demonstrated the existence of invisible intelligences beyond those of the people who were sitting at the time in the room.

One method of claimed communication is that which is called "independent writing," either on paper or upon slates. I have experimented a great many times in this direction. I believe that nearly all that which is called slate-writing is fraud, and that most "slate-writing mediums" had better be severely let alone. But I have known a few cases which, with all the study I have been able to give to them, I have not been able to explain as fraudulent. I have not treated the matter carelessly, for in the course of my investigation I have discovered and exposed several fraudulent "mediums" of this class. But once in my life I obtained writing on my own slate, holding it in my own hands, without the psychic's having touched it or having had anything to do with it whatsoever. I simply state this as a fact, and leave people to explain it if they can.

I will mention one other strange case of slate-writing, which was told me by a friend in whom I have the utmost confidence. And this confidence perhaps others will share with me the more readily when I tell them that he was and is now an utter unbeliever in any communications from the other world ; indeed, he does not believe in any other world, and says that he does not want to. He is a Jewish rabbi. He told me that he went to a slate-writing " medium " in Chicago—the account of this he gave me immediately after his return. He said that he wrote a brief note to his father, who had died years before in Germany. He wrote the note in German, spelling it out with Hebrew characters. This he did to preclude the possibility of the " medium's " knowing what it was, even if she had some surreptitious way of reading it. He said that he then placed this note between two slates of his own, tied them together, and at the direction of the psychic hung them on the chandelier over the table where they were sitting. After a little time he was directed to take them down and open them. On the inside he found, written on the slate, a reply to his note, signed by his father's name, and written in precisely the same way in which he had written his own —that is, in the German language, but spelled with Hebrew characters.

I have had a good deal of experience with what is called automatic writing. In most of these cases I have been told of things which I knew beforehand. In a few, the things communicated to me I did not know, and it was not possible that the psychic should have known.

A young man in a city not more than twenty miles from Boston, a clerk in a manufactory, wrote me that he found himself seized with this impulse to write, that he did not understand it, and that he wished to come and talk it over with me. I set a day and hour for his visit. He sat in my study in the church (this was when I was living in Boston), my house being perhaps three quarters of a mile away. I had never seen the young man before, and he was entirely unknown to any of my family. He sat down, and his hand began to write. The communications were signed by the name of a man who claimed to have lived and died in the city of Philadelphia. I asked him certain questions about himself, and as far as I was able to carry out my inquiry the answers he made were correct. It occurred to me then to try a little test. I said, speaking to the supposed invisible communicator, " Would it be possible for you to go anywhere in the city, while I am sitting here, and find out some fact, and come back and tell me about it ? " The answer was that he had never tried to do such a thing, but he saw no reason why he should not, and he would try anything I might suggest. I asked him then if he would be kind enough to go over to my house, find out where Mrs. Savage was and what she was doing, and come back and let me know. When I had left for my study in the morning, she had told me that she expected to be away from the house during the forenoon, but would be back in time for lunch. I mention this because on the theory of auto-suggestion or telepathy it is frequently said that when you sit with a psychic you get what you are expecting for an answer. I pulled my watch out and waited, between three and four minutes, in perfect silence. At the end of that time the hand began to write again, and, entirely contrary to my expectation, I was informed that Mrs. Savage was at home, and that when the intelligence, writing, was there, she was standing in the front hall, saying good-bye to a caller. When I got home I asked her if she had been out, as she expected. She answered, with a good deal of disgust, that she had not ; that she had been flooded with people who had called on her for one reason or another all the morning, and had not been able to get a minute for the things she had intended to do. Then I said, "Where were you at half-past eleven?"—just the time when this communication was made to me. She thought a minute, and then, with a look of annoyance on her face, said, "Indeed, I know where I was then. A woman on some mission from the South had been here for a long while, until I was bored and tired to death, and at half-past eleven I was standing in the hall and wishing that she would go." This she said she was sure of because she happened to glance at the clock on the parlor mantel while she was standing there, and saw the hands pointing to that hour.

One more instance I will give, again a little one, for which I can find no ordinary explanation. I have a friend, a widow, living on Massachusetts Avenue in Boston. She has an intimate friend living on Beacon Street at the Back Bay. This friend at the Back Bay, though nobody but a few intimates were familiar with it, was sensitive to psychic influences, and used to get, or think that she got, communications from the father of her friend on Massachusetts Avenue. The incident that occurred was this: the Massachusetts Avenue lady received a letter from her friend in Beacon

Street, asking her to come over and dine with
her on the following Monday. This was in
the middle of the previous week. When my
friend received the letter she said to herself,
" I cannot accept this invitation to dinner, because I am already engaged for that evening."
She was accustomed to be an early riser, and
to write her letters before breakfast and hand
them to the carrier when he delivered the mail
about eight o'clock in the morning, so as to
save herself the trouble of going out. The
next morning, waking early, she was thinking
that she must get up and reply to this letter,
when the thought came into her mind, " Now
if father does really communicate with her,
why cannot he tell her that I am engaged next
Monday night?" And she said it seemed to
her that if he would do so it would be a pretty
good test of the reality of the claim. She got
up and wrote the letter and gave it to the
carrier to be put into the mail. Familiar as I
was for years with the times of the delivery of
mails in Boston, I know that this letter could
not have reached the friend in Beacon Street
earlier than noon, and judged by my own experience the chances were that it would not
reach her before the three-o'clock delivery in
the afternoon. But (and now comes the strange

thing about it) at half-past ten, or earlier than that, the coachman of the Beacon Street lady appeared in Massachusetts Avenue with a note saying, "You need not take the trouble to answer my letter of yesterday, because your father has been here and has told me you cannot come to dinner Monday night."

Now, for one or two cases of personal experience. I carried on for a long time a series of sittings in my study in Boston, the psychic in the case being one of my parishioners, a friend whom I had known for years. She never sat for money, and could not have been induced to sit with a stranger under any conditions. Sitting in this way, I was told over and over and over again things with which my friend could by no possibility have been acquainted. The communications were of various kinds, most of them, however, being through automatic writing. Her hand would write, while we were sitting and talking about some subject entirely foreign to that with which the hand was engaged, and while she was apparently in a perfectly normal condition.

One day there claimed to be present a friend of mine who had lived and died in the State of Maine, and whom I had intimately known in my youth, but whom I had seen only rarely in

later years. She had been dead about five or
six months at this time. I was not thinking
of her as I was sitting on this particular morning, when suddenly the hand began to write,
and two pages of note paper were covered,
addressed to me, but not signed. I took it up
and read it, thinking to myself that if such a
thing were possible I would take my oath that
this was a note from the friend referred to
above. And let me say here that the friend
who was acting as psychic not only was not acquainted with the friend who had died, but
had never known that any such person had
ever existed in the universe. After reading
the note I said, " Will not whoever has written this note be kind enough to give me the
name ?"—and at once the name was written,
maiden name and married name. Then we
began a conversation which lasted an hour, as
natural and intelligible as conversation between
any two friends could be. I asked questions
about her family, her children, and her sisters ;
asked her if she remembered books that we
used to read together years and years ago, before either of us was married, and she gave me
the names of them. I asked her if she remembered one particular poem of which we were
both very fond, and she gave the name of that.

And so the conversation went on. But I put this all aside, as lacking in sufficiency of proof; for I said to myself, " I know all these things, nothing has been told me that I did not know, and I have been wishing that I might be told things which I did not know." These I was always looking for.

A week later (for we were holding these sittings once a week) she claimed to be present again, when I asked of her a similar test to one referred to above. I asked her if she could go or send to the State of Maine and find out where her sister was and what she was doing, while we were sitting there. She said she would try. In less than fifteen minutes, after a perfect silence, the hand of the psychic began to write, and I was informed as to where the sister was and what she was doing. This again was entirely contrary to my expectations, because there were reasons which would have led me to suppose that on this particular day this sister, whom I had known for years but very rarely saw, was in another town. I wrote to her, and found out by return mail that the news given me in my study in Boston was precisely correct.

The next week a still more strange and startling thing occurred. I had known the sister referred to ever since I was fifteen or sixteen years of age. I knew she was married and living in Maine. I had not seen her for years; I do not know that I had ever seen her husband. I had no reason to suppose that they were not living together in perfect accord and happiness. Suddenly on the third morning, my friend began to speak about her sister. She said, "She is exceedingly unhappy, is passing through the greatest sorrow of her life. I wish I could make her know that I care. I wish you would write to her for me." I asked what the matter was, for I knew absolutely nothing about the situation of affairs. There was a distinct hesitancy, as though she did not quite know whether to speak of the situation before a third person — that, at any rate was the impression made on my mind. At last, however, as though seeing no other way, she told me that the cause was the infidelity and cruelty of the sister's husband. All this was an utter surprise to me; and again let me repeat that the psychic, before these sittings began, did not know that there were any such people in the world. I asked her to tell me what she wished to about the matter, which she did. I then sat down and wrote a letter to the sister, asking her if she was in any special trouble, and if so, and the nature of it was such that she could, if she would tell me about it. I received by return mail a letter marked "Private and Confidential," in which every syllable that had been told me was confirmed as true ; and I was begged, the minute I had read the letter, to burn it, because, as she said, if her husband knew she had written any such letter he would kill her.

These last, as well as some of the others above referred to, are specimens of cases which I am not able to explain on any of the theories which have been advocated which fall short of communication from some invisible intelligence. I do not hold my opinions in any dogmatic fashion. I am ready to revise or surrender any one of my present beliefs if some adequate reason can be given me for so doing. But none of the explanations which have ever been offered to me—and I have read almost everything that I could get which has been written in this direction—have seemed to me adequate. It certainly was not fraud. It certainly was not auto-suggestion on the part of either of us, for both of us were in absolute ignorance of the facts. It does not seem to me that telepathy can explain it, for the conditions which accompany telepathy were entirely absent. I

cannot yet accept the theory—supported by
some—that the psychic unconsciously dips the
bewildering variety of unknown facts out of
the limitless ocean of the universal mind. And
I confess that I can see no reasonable explanation excepting the supposition that my dead
friend was there and actually told me these
things. When somebody can give me an adequate explanation of the facts in some other direction, I shall be ready to consider and adopt
it if the evidence seems to point that way.

I give these cases because they are outside
of those which have been published in connection with the investigations of the Society for
Psychical Research. I was a corporate member of that society, and have been in sympathy
with it and working with it since it was first
organised. But while I have been working as
a member of that society, and sometimes as
connected with some of its committees, I have
always been carrying on quiet private investigations on my own account ; and I have given
here some specimens of such things as I have
found.

I know, as well as I know my existence,
that the things I have here set down are true.
I have discovered in the last twenty-five years
no end of fraud. I have discovered any

amount of delusion and self-deception. I have found people claiming to be "mediums" who have had some strange experiences, but who, as it seems to me, did not need to go outside this world for an explanation of them. I have attended any number of "dark seances," but have never used anything which occurred in them as evidence, not because a good many of the things may not have been true, but because even the honest investigator is so liable to be deceived in regard to things which take place under such conditions. I have put aside always anything, however strange it may have seemed to me, of which I was not absolutely sure, and of which I did not make a record at the time. I have attended a good many so-called "materialising seances," but there has always been something the matter with them. I have never been able to be certain as to what was going on ; and consequently I have never counted them as testimony. Indeed, I am inclined to think that all of them are fraudulent.

Let me add one thing more, for the sake of explaining my personal attitude and the method I follow. I have never, with one exception, attempted to get any communication from any particular friend or person. I have been governed by no prurient curiosity or love for the mystic or marvellous. I have simply been engaged in trying to find out whether certain alleged things were true, and, if they were true, what their bearing might be on the nature of man and the possibility of continued existence. In these inquiries I have followed the most rigid scientific method. I have kept nothing which was doubtful, nothing which I have not seen and known and demonstrated to be true.

As the result of my study, I cannot help feeling that we are on the eve of discovering the Other Country, as really as Columbus discovered America. Of course, I shall be glad, as countless thousands and millions of other people will be, if this shall prove to be so. I confess that I am inclined to agree with Dr. Hodgson, the Secretary of the Society for Psychical Research ; with Mr. Frederic W. H. Myers, the great essayist in England ; with Professor Lodge, the physicist and mathematician of the old British Association ; and with a great many others who have carefully studied the matter, that continued existence, and at least occasional communication, are already demonstrated.

I submit at any rate that, as Mr. Gladstone says, and as a good many others have said a hundred times before he said it (I mention

him because great names do count with people)
that *this is the most important subject of study
in the world.* It ought to be settled, one way
or the other—settled beyond dispute. And I,
for one, am ready to say that I will bow my
head loyally to any competent settlement, whatever it may be. If, when I get through with
this life, that is the end of me, I would rather
know it now, and adjust my life to facts, rather
than to imaginary conditions. If it shall be
proved true, as I hope it may, that we continue
to exist, and, in accordance with the facts of
evolution, to advance toward ever higher and
nobler conditions, I shall be glad to have done
ever so little in helping to establish this magnificent and inspiring truth.

INDEX

Abbott, Dr. Lyman, 194

Accordion, played by invisible agency, 302–304

Agnosticism, a product of scientific thought, 165 ; definition of the word, 170–172 ; false, 173 ; real, 173–175 ; prevalence of, to-day, 176

Agnostics, real truth-seekers, 173–175 ; often the noblest men, 176

Ahriman, the principle of darkness and evil in Persian theology, 34

Aldrich, on Bayard Taylor's death, 183

Apparitions, of the dead, cases personally known to author, 308–312

Arguments, usual, in favour of future life, deceptive, 230

Author not a Spiritualist, 312–313 ; earnest, scientific investigator, 326 *ff.*

Automatic writing, author's experiences with, 316–319, 321–325 ; case of, reported by author's friend, 319–321 ; author unable to explain, 325 ; except on the ground of communication from the dead, 326

Auto-suggestion, theory of, 318–325

Awakening, author's first, to the importance of studying spiritualistic phenomena, 296–298

Belief in future life, of primitive men, 9–18 ; of ancient Egyptians, 22, 25 ; of Scandinavians, 22 ; of Indians, 23 ; of Persians, *ib.* ; of Greeks and Romans, 23–28, 31–32 ; of the majority of men, not evidence, not proof, 228 *ff.* ; never scientifically investigated till 1882, 248 *ff.*

Body, is man only a? 213 *ff.*

Brahma, absorption in, final aim of Brahmins' wishes, 30

Brahmins, their horror of reincarnation, 29, 30

Browning, on immortality, 182–183

Buddhists, their horror of reincarnation, 29, 30

Church, the, stops intellectual advance, 161 ; spiritual tyranny of, in the Middle Ages, 161–163 ; the Renaissance a reaction against, 163 *ff.* ; her abuse of the word "faith," 166 *ff.*; attitude of, towards the Spiritualist movement, 187–188 ; only spiritual power in the Middle Ages, 214 ; hostile to scientific inquiry, 245 *ff.*

Clairvoyance and clairaudience established beyond question, 307

Clarke, Dr., of Boston, on visions of the dying, 309

Communications, with the dead possible, 265 *ff.* ; inexplicable, save through psychics, 314–326; from the dead only probable explanation of certain facts, 326 ; demonstrated in the opinion of many eminent men, 328

Copernicus, his theory of the universe known to Milton, 135–136

Dante, his great poem constructed on the Ptolemaic theory of the universe and on mediæval theology, 113–124 ; general impression it leaves on the average reader, 125–132

Dead, the, are they alive? 265 *ff.* ; communication with, possible, *ib.* ; apparitions of, 308–312; communication f r o m, only possible explanation of certain facts, 326

Death, is it the end or a new beginning? 2 ; importance of the question, 2–6 ; ideas of primitive men on, 8–18 ; of later races, 32–35 ; looked upon as a calamity, 65 ; desired by Paul and Socrates, 63, 66–67 ; conquered by Christ, 78, 85 *ff.*, 88 ; denied by advanced psychics, 265 *ff.* ; not painful, 271 ; not a violent change, 272

Doubt pervades the Church and the world, 202–210

Easter, Christian, its significance, 178 ; the same as that claimed for Spiritualism, 179

Egyptians, ancient, their ideas of the soul's course after death, 22 ; of a dual soul, 25

Elysium, the place for the good in the underworld of the Greeks and Romans, 35

Essenes, Hebrew Platonists, 60

Experiences, author's personal, 295 *ff.* (Appendix) ; first, with raps and table-tipping, 295 ; with furniture, 301 ; with accordion, 302–304 ; later, with raps, 305–306 ; with telepathy, 307–308 ; apparitions of the dead, 308–312 ; with visions of the dying, 310–311 ; with inexplicable communications through psychics, 314–326 ; with slate-writing, 315 ; with automatic writing, 316–319, 321–326 ; with frauds, 326–327

Faith, abuse of the word by the Church, 166 *ff.* ; Paul's definition of, 167 ; true meaning of, 168, 169 ; not evidence, not proof, 228

Friends, our, in the spirit world, probably near us, 281 *ff.* ; interfere only occasionally, 284–287 ; probably ministering spirits, 284, 291–292

Gautama (Buddha), 30

Gehenna, the place of punishment in Sheol or the underworld, 58–59, 72, 95–96

Ghosts, *see* Apparitions

Gladstone, on the work of the Society for Psychical Research, 253–254 ; on the all-importance of the study of psychical phenomena, 254

Greek philosophy, scientific tendency of, 160 ; revival of, 163 *f.*

Greeks and Romans, their ideas of future life, 23–28, 31–32 ; on death, 35

Hades, the Greek name for the underworld, hell, sheol, 58

Heathens, all consigned to hell by the churches, 146–148

Heaven, in the Old Testament, 45–46 ; difficulty of locating, 142–145 ; who is to go to, 149 ; unsatisfactory pictures of life in, 150 *ff.*

Hebrews, originally nature-wor-shippers, 52 ; take little thought of a future life at first, 53 ; originate the idea of resur-rection, 56–57 ; their moral evolution, 58–62

" Hell," in the Old Testament, 47–52 (*see* Sheol), 55, 56 ; in Dante's poem, 121–123 ; diffi-culty of locating, 142–145

Hillis, Dr., successor of Dr. Lyman Abbott at Plymouth Church, 194

Holmes, Oliver Wendell, on im-mortality, 134 ; on visions of the dying, 309

Home, the Spiritualist medium, experiments with, 302

Huxley, created the names "ag-nostic" and "agnosticism," 170 ; on materialism, 237

Hydesville, N. Y., birthplace of modern Spiritualism, 185

Hypnotism, the modern name for Mesmerism, 256

Immortality, belief in, inborn in man, 10 *ff.* ; universal among great civilised races, 20 *ff.* ; yet said to have been first brought to light by Christ, 88–89

Indians believe in heavens and hells, 23

Jesus, his opinions difficult to ascertain, easy to misrepre-sent, 89–93 ; his reticence on several important questions, 93 *ff.* ; his teaching of the kingdom of heaven and of eternal life not dogmatic, but entirely human, 102–106

Job, Book of, its ethical charac-ter, 54

Life, future, ideas of primitive men on, 8–18 ; of ancient Egyptians, 22, 25 ; of Scandi-navians, 22 ; of Indians, 23 ; of Persians, *ib.* ; of Greeks

and Romans, 23–28, 31–32 ; has no part in the Mosaic tra-dition, 43 *ff.* ; as vaguely im-agined by the Hebrews, 44 –57 ; vaguely indicated by Jesus, 97 *ff.* ; belief in, exag-gerated, 180 ; attitude of poets towards belief in, 181–185 ; proofs of, passionately desired, 220 *ff.* ; probabilities in favour of, 224 *ff.*

Livermore, Mrs. Mary A. ; her experience with a warning " voice," 285

Longfellow, on death, 182

Lucifer, his rebellion, 69, 117

Man, beginnings of, 241 ; evolu-tion of, 242, 243

Materialism, dangers of, 217 *ff.* ; growth of, 237 ; decay and death of, among scientific men, 237–238

Mediums, foolish to consult them, 196 *f.* ; necessary agents of transmission, like telegraph wires, 282–284 ; slate-writing, frequently frauds, 315

Mesmer, 256 ; his discoveries, ridiculed by contemporary sci-entists, proved true by later science, 306–307

Messages, spiritualistic, vary in character and value, 195–198

Middle Ages, the, a time of spiritual darkness and horror, 111 ; theory of the universe in, 112–114 ; embodied in Dante's poem, 114, 124 ; characteris-tic beliefs of, 157–160 ; their supposed knowledge of the other world, 158–160 ; their ignorance of this world, *ib.* ; tyrannised by the Church, 161 –163

Milton, acquainted with the Co-pernican system, but clings to the Ptolemaic, 135–136 ; theo-logical framework of his epic, 137–138

Mind-reading, a fact personally known to author, 307, 308; insufficient to account for certain facts, 314

Moses, his Egyptian education, 42; leaves out of his legislation the Egyptian teaching of a future life, 42 *ff*.

Mystery surrounding us an incentive and hope, not a reason for discouragement, 293, 294

Nirvana, object of Buddha's desire, 30

Norsemen, *see* Scandinavians

Old Testament, vague on the subject of future life, 43-52; attaches no idea of reward and punishment to it, 54

Other country, the, discovery of, imminent, 328; existence of, already demonstrated in the opinion of many eminent men, *ib*.

Paradise, the place of reward in sheol, or the underworld, 58, 59, 72, 95, 96; in Dante's poem, 124, 130

Parker, Theodore, at Thoreau's deathbed, 1; his consciousness of immortality, 227; his argument from the misery of the present life, 230

Paul, prefers death to life, 63, 68; his scheme of the world and the universe and his belief in the Messiah before his conversion, 69-73; his change of faith, 73; his doctrine of Christ's second advent, 74-77; of resurrection, 77-80; of universal salvation, 82, 83; his unworldliness (Christian stoicism), 83-85; commends spirit of inquiry, 245

Persians, ancient, believe in heavens and hells, 23; their theology based on duality—good and evil, 34

Pharisees, the Hebrew majority at the time of Christ, believing in immortality and hosts of spirits, good and evil, 60, 61

Phelps, Professor, at Andover attests reality of phenomena, 186; striking phenomena in his father's house in Connecticut, 299-300

Power, evolution of, from muscular to spiritual, 242-243; not physical, producing physical effects; what is it? 299

Probabilities and intuitions in favour of future life, 224 *ff*.

Protestants, oppose science and independent thought as bitterly as the Catholic Church, 141; equally deny the salvation of virtuous heathens and infants dead before the advent of Christ, 146-148; all teach doctrine of eternal punishment, 148-149

Psychical Research, the Society for, its institution and membership, 251-253; Gladstone's attitude towards, 253-254; its aims and work, 254 *ff*.; its field of research, 257-259

Ptolemaic scheme of the universe, accepted in the Middle Ages, 114-117; accepted by Dante as the framework of his poem, 113 *ff*.; and by Milton, 136

Punishment, eternal; did Jesus believe in it? 99; doctrine of, impious and blasphemous, 101, 131; taught by all churches, 148-149

Purgatory in Dante's poem, 124

Rappings and physical manifestations defended, 194 *ff*.; author's first experiences with, 295; later, 305-306; difficulty in explaining, 306

Reason, said to be incompatible with religious dogma, 246

Reincarnation, belief in and horror of, of Brahmins and Buddhists, 28–31

Renaissance, the, a reaction against the intellectual tyranny of the Church, 163 *ff.*

Resurrection, true original meaning of the word, 56, 80 ; Paul's doctrine of, 77–80 ; of the body, not believed in by Paul, 79, taught by the churches, 125, 152 *f.* ; of the body of Christ, evidence for, unsatisfactory, 200 *ff.*

Rome, ancient, her attitude towards Christians political, not religious, 86 ; how conquered by Christians, 87 ; Christian, her power in the Middle Ages, 214

Sadducees, Hebrew conservatives, with no belief in a future life, 59

Satan, in Dante's poem, 117–118, 123

Scandinavians, their ideas of blessedness in Valhalla, 22

Scepticism, rise of, as the protest of the best minds against priestly fictions and claims, 37 *ff.*

Senses, the physical, sometimes dispensed with, 264 ; knowledge arrived at through other channels than, 267 *ff.* ; their limitations, 277–279

Sheol, the Hebrew name for hell, the underworld, hades, 48, 50

Slate-writing, frequently fraud, 315 ; author's personal experience of, apparently genuine, *ib.* ; case of genuine, reported by author's friend, 316

Socrates, his friendly view of death, 66–67

Soul, is man a? 209 *ff.* ; personal, conscious existence of, not proven, 239

Souls, unhappy state of, in the underworld, according to ancient Greeks and Romans, 26, 31, 32

Spencer, Herbert, on intuitions in favour of future life, 226

Spirit photographs scientifically possible, 279–280

Spirit-world, the, nearness of, in the Gospel, 108–110

Spiritualism, significance claimed for it, 179 ; a reaction against agnostic science, 181 ; its beginnings, 185–186 ; unfavourably regarded by churches, 187 *ff.* ; manifestations of, at the beginnings of all great religions, 188–190 ; its own worst enemy, 191 ; discredited by " fakes and frauds," 193, 303 ; ethics of, noble and lofty, 198

Spiritualists, their excessive credulity, 191 ; timidity, 192–193 ; certain, Spiritualism's worst enemies, 313

Study of spiritualistic phenomena, importance of, first realised by author, 296–298 ; the one all-important, 329

Subliminal consciousness, 257

Tables and other furniture, extraordinary performances of, 299–301

Table-tipping, 295, 299

Tartarus, the place of punishment in the underworld of the Greeks and Romans, 35

Telepathy, what it is, 262–263 ; established beyond question, 307 ; not yet explained, 308 ; insufficient to explain certain facts, 314

Tennyson, on future life, 182

Theosophy, modern name alleged to embody some of Buddha's ideas, 24

Tyndall, on the brain, 238

Underworld, the, or world of the dead, as imagined by the

Underworld—*Continued*
Greeks and Romans, 23 *ff.*, 26 *ff.*, 35 ; by the Hebrews, 47, 52, 55–56 (*see* sheol) ; divided into place of reward and of punishment — Paradise a n d Gehenna, 58, 61, 72 ; the place where all go, good and bad, 71–72, 80, 89
Universalist doctrine held by Paul, 82
Universe, history of, 239 *ff.*

Valhalla, the S c a n d i n a v i a n heaven for the souls of brave warriors, 22
Visions of the dying, 309–311
Wallace, Alfred Russel, his ex-perience w i t h spirit photo-graphy, 279–280
Walt Whitman, on future life 184
Wesley Family, disturbed by spiritualistic manifestations, 185–186 ; striking phenomena in their house, 299–300
Whittier, on death, and spirit world, 181–182
World, the other, not strange or lonely, 273, nothing known about, 273–275 ; w h e r e i s it? 275–277 ; invisible and intangi-ble, yet real, 277–279 ; life in. what is it like ? 287 *ff.* ; value of earthly gifts and training in, *ib.*
Writing, slate, 315–316 ; auto-matic, 316–326

By W. M. RAMSAY.

THE CHURCH IN THE ROMAN EMPIRE BEFORE A.D. 170.

With Maps and Illustrations, 8vo $3.00

"It is a book of very exceptional value, Prof. Ramsay is a real scholar and of the very best type of scholarship. A thoroughly good book ; a product of first-hand and accurate scholarship ; in the highest degree suggestive ; and not only valuable in its results, but an admirable example of the true method of research."—*The Churchman.*

ST. PAUL THE TRAVELLER AND THE ROMAN CITIZEN.

With Map, 8vo $3.00

"A work which marks an important step in advance in the historical interpretation of St. Paul. . . . It is an immense gain to have the narrative lifted from the mean function of being an artful monument and mirror of a strife internal to Christianity which it seeks by a process, now of creation, now of elimination, to overcome and to conceal, to the high purpose of representing the religion as it began within the Empire and as it actually was to the Empire and the Empire to it. . . . Professor Ramsay has made a solid and valuable contribution to the interpretation of the Apostolic literature and of the Apostolic age—a contribution distinguished no less by ripe scholarship, independent judgment, keen vision, and easy mastery of material, than by freshness of thought, boldness of combination, and striking originality of view."—*The Speaker.*

IMPRESSIONS OF TURKEY DURING TWELVE YEARS' WANDERINGS.

8vo $1.75

"No conception of the real status of Turkey is possible unless something is understood of 'the interlacing and alternation of the separate and unblending races.' . . . Such an understanding is admirably presented in Prof. Ramsay's book, which gives a near and trustworthy insight into actual Turkish conditions."—*N. Y. Times.*

WAS CHRIST BORN AT BETHLEHEM?

A Study in the Credibility of St. Luke. Part I. The Importance of the Problem. Part II. The Solution of the Problem. 8vo, $1.75

"The work is one of which students of biblical criticism will need to take account. It is absolutely candid and straightforward, thorough and discriminating, and courteous to other scholars whose conclusions it sees most reason to condemn. It is a fine piece of work."—*The Congregationalist.*

HISTORICAL COMMENTARY UPON THE EPISTLE TO THE GALATIANS.

8vo $1.75

G. P. PUTNAM'S SONS, New York and London.